POTATO COOKERY

Hamlyn Cookshelf Series

Potato Cookery

Linda Collister

Hamlyn
London · New York · Sydney · Toronto

The publishers would like to thank the Potato Marketing Board
for all their help and information.

Cover photograph by James Jackson
Photography by David Johnson

Line drawings by Robin Lawrie

First published in 1984 by
The Hamlyn Publishing Group Limited
London · New York · Sydney · Toronto
Astronaut House, Feltham, Middlesex, England
© Copyright The Hamlyn Publishing Group Limited 1984

ISBN 0 600 32329 3 (hardback)
0 600 32419 2 (softback)

Set in Monophoto Rockwell
by Servis Filmsetting Limited, Manchester, England

Printed in Yugoslavia

Contents

Useful Facts and Figures

Notes on metrication

In this book quantities are given in metric and Imperial measures. Exact conversion from Imperial to metric measures does not usually give very convenient working quantities and so the metric measures have been rounded off into units of 25 grams. The table below shows the recommended equivalents.

Ounces	Approx g to nearest whole figure	Recommended conversion to nearest unit of 25	Ounces	Approx g to nearest whole figure	Recommended conversion to nearest unit of 25
1	28	25	11	312	300
2	57	50	12	340	350
3	85	75	13	368	375
4	113	100	14	396	400
5	142	150	15	425	425
6	170	175	16 (1 lb)	454	450
7	198	200	17	482	475
8	227	225	18	510	500
9	255	250	19	539	550
10	283	275	20 ($1\frac{1}{4}$ lb)	567	575

Note: When converting quantities over 20 oz first add the appropriate figures in the centre column, then adjust to the nearest unit of 25. As a general guide, 1 kg (1000 g) equals 2.2 lb or about 2 lb 3 oz. This method of conversion gives good results in nearly all cases, although in certain pastry and cake recipes a more accurate conversion is necessary to produce a balanced recipe.

Liquid measures The millilitre has been used in this book and the following table gives a few examples.

Imperial	Approx ml to nearest whole figure	Recommended ml	Imperial	Approx ml to nearest whole figure	Recommended ml
$\frac{1}{4}$ pint	142	150 ml	1 pint	567	600 ml
$\frac{1}{2}$ pint	283	300 ml	$1\frac{1}{2}$ pints	851	900 ml
$\frac{3}{4}$ pint	425	450 ml	$1\frac{3}{4}$ pints	992	1000 ml (1 litre)

Spoon measures All spoon measures given in this book are level unless otherwise stated.

Can sizes At present, cans are marked with the exact (usually to the nearest whole number) metric equivalent of the Imperial weight of the contents, so we have followed this practice when giving can sizes.

Oven temperatures

The table below gives recommended equivalents.

	°C	°F	Gas Mark		°C	°F	Gas Mark
Very cool	110	225	$\frac{1}{4}$	Moderately hot	190	375	5
	120	250	$\frac{1}{2}$		200	400	6
Cool	140	275	1	Hot	220	425	7
	150	300	2		230	450	8
Moderate	160	325	3	Very hot	240	475	9
	180	350	4				

Notes for American and Australian users

In America the 8-fl oz measuring cup is used. In Australia metric measures are now used in conjunction with the standard 250-ml measuring cup. The Imperial pint, used in Britain and Australia, is 20 fl oz, while the American pint is 16 fl oz. It is important to remember that the Australian tablespoon differs from both the British and American tablespoons; the table below gives a comparison. The British standard tablespoon, which has been used throughout this book, holds 17.7 ml, the American 14.2 ml, and the Australian 20 ml. A teaspoon holds approximately 5 ml in all three countries.

British	American	Australian
1 teaspoon	1 teaspoon	1 teaspoon
1 tablespoon	1 tablespoon	1 tablespoon
2 tablespoons	3 tablespoons	2 tablespoons
$3\frac{1}{2}$ tablespoons	4 tablespoons	3 tablespoons
4 tablespoons	5 tablespoons	$3\frac{1}{2}$ tablespoons

An Imperial/American guide to solid and liquid measures

Imperial	American	Imperial	American
Solid measures		**Liquid measures**	
1 lb butter or		$\frac{1}{4}$ pint liquid	$\frac{2}{3}$ cup liquid
margarine	2 cups	$\frac{1}{2}$ pint	$1\frac{1}{4}$ cups
1 lb flour	4 cups	$\frac{3}{4}$ pint	2 cups
1 lb granulated		1 pint	$2\frac{1}{2}$ cups
or caster sugar	2 cups	$1\frac{1}{2}$ pints	$3\frac{3}{4}$ cups
1 lb icing sugar	3 cups	2 pints	5 cups ($2\frac{1}{2}$ pints)
8 oz rice	1 cup		

NOTE: WHEN MAKING ANY OF THE RECIPES IN THIS BOOK, ONLY FOLLOW ONE SET OF MEASURES AS THEY ARE NOT INTERCHANGEABLE.

Introduction

Thank Heaven for potatoes! I don't know what we would do without them for they hold a very important place in our diet. Potato consumption has increased in recent years and the British, for example, are now eating an average of 105 kg/230 lb of potatoes per person per year – more than ever before.

History

Life without potatoes in one form or another is hard to imagine, but they have only been eaten in Europe for the last 250 years. Potatoes originated in the Andes and have been part of the staple diet of the South American Peruvians for many thousands of years. They were first brought to Europe in 1538 by the Spanish explorer Sieza de Leon, and they were initially cultivated as ornamental plants. From Spain the potato was gradually introduced to Germany via central Europe, and the first potato was said to have been brought to England by Sir John Hawkins in 1563. However, potatoes were largely ignored at first despite the endeavours of Sir Francis Drake and Sir Walter Raleigh; Raleigh grew potatoes on his estate in Ireland and persuaded the Irish to cultivate them.

The potato had reached France by about 1665 but it was treated with suspicion and not cultivated due to a fear of leprosy. Antoine-Auguste Parmentier, an eighteenth-century scientist interested in nutrition, realised the food value of potatoes and tried to popularize them. He gave a bunch of potato flowers to Louis XVI for Marie-Antoinette to wear in her hair. Louis also wore a potato flower as a buttonflower, and potatoes and potato flowers thus became a status symbol at the French court. To this day in France many dishes containing potatoes are named after Parmentier.

By the end of the eighteenth century potatoes had become a staple crop in Germany and Ireland. When blight attacked the 1847 potato crop in Ireland there was mass starvation and $1\frac{1}{2}$

million people emigrated to America. The United States is now the world's largest potato producer and the potato is second only to rice as a food crop.

Food Value

Why are potatoes so popular? An obvious reason is their low cost – potatoes are wonderful value for money – but they are also highly nutritious. Potatoes contain some protein, carbohydrate, calcium, iron and sodium – minerals essential to our diet – as well as vitamins C, the B group and fibre. On average, people in Europe eat 200 g/7 oz of potato per person each day, which provides about 4% of our protein intake, 8% of our iron intake and 24% of our vitamin C intake. Additionally, a 200-g/7-oz potato baked in its skin provides 16% of our daily fibre requirement. And potatoes needn't be fattening. Use a dressing of chives with yogurt or cottage cheese on a baked potato instead of the more usual butter, soured cream or full fat cheese; bake or boil potatoes in their skins instead of frying or roasting them in calorie-laden fat. Give your heart a break as well as your figure!

Nutritional Content per 100 g/4 oz

	Raw	Boiled	Chipped	Roasted
Energy Value kJ	318	331	989	515
Kcal	76	79	236	123
Protein g	2.1	1.4	3.8	2.8
Fat g	0	0	9.0	1.0
Carbohydrate g	18.0	19.7	37.3	27.3
Calcium mg	8.0	4	10	10
Iron mg	0.7	0.5	1.0	1.0
Thiamine mg	0.11	0.08	0.10	0.10
Riboflavin mg	0.04	0.03	0.04	0.04
Nicotinic acid total mg	1.2	0.8	1.2	1.2
Equivalents mg	1.8	1.2	2.2	2.0
Vitamin C mg	8–30	4–15	6–20	6–23
(Vitamin C falls during storage)				

As well as being cheap and nutritious potatoes are also extremely versatile, in fact there seems to be no end to the number of ways potatoes can be served. The *Larousse Gastronomique* lists over one hundred ways of serving the potato and, as this little book shows, potatoes can be used to make pancakes, bread and pastry doughs, sponge cakes and puddings, fritter batter, a choux-type pastry, gnocchi, sweets, biscuits – the list seems endless!

Useful Tips

Here are a few tips to help you get the best from your potatoes. Avoid any potatoes which are:
- not correctly graded for size: if larger than 8 cm/3 in. in diameter they should be sold as baking potatoes, and if smaller than 4 cm/1½ in. they should be sold as new potatoes or 'mids';
- affected by common scab on more than a quarter of the surface;
- unsound, dirty or muddy;
- tainted, damaged, diseased or with spade marks;
- badly misshapen, shrivelled or wizened;
- bruised or damaged by frosts or pests;
- affected by greening, hollow heart or water logging.

It's best to buy new potatoes in small quantities because they taste nicest fresh from the ground. Eat them as soon as possible and avoid storing them for longer than two days because after that they start to lose their wonderful flavour. To test how fresh potatoes are in a shop, rub them gently – the skins should come off easily and the potatoes should be slightly damp to the touch.

If you normally use more than 3.25 kg/7 lb of potatoes each week it's best to buy them in bulk. The 6.25-kg/14-lb or 13.5-kg/28-lb brown paper sacks available in some shops are considerably cheaper than loose potatoes. Be careful to store potatoes in a cool, dry, dark airy place; they may turn green if exposed to the light and any green spots must be cut out before use because they taste unpleasant. Potatoes turn black when they have caught the frost and must be destroyed. Conditions which are too warm, however, cause potatoes to sprout – the ideal storage temperature is around 5–10 C/45–50 F. Don't store potatoes in polythene bags because the condensation makes them damp, which causes them to rot. Potatoes also bruise easily, so handle them with care!

You will benefit, too, from preparing and cooking potatoes carefully. If you have to peel potatoes, peel them very thinly using a sharp peeler or a special vegetable knife – this will reduce the vitamin loss. Cut maincrop or old potatoes into even-sized pieces for cooking; this means they will all be cooked at the same time and you won't get a few small, broken soggy potatoes in a pan of rock-hard larger ones. Try not to peel potatoes too far in advance because they turn brown when exposed to the air. Immediately cover peeled potatoes with plenty of cold water.

The best way to avoid boiled potatoes disintegrating or going soggy during cooking is to cook them as follows: put them in a pan of cold, salted water to cover. Cover the pan with a lid and put over a high heat until the water boils. Then reduce the heat and allow the water to simmer gently. If the potatoes are boiled too fast, the outsides will break up while the centre is uncooked. If your potatoes tend to go black or brown during cooking, add a teaspoon of vinegar or lemon juice to the water. Above all, don't waste the water in which you have cooked potatoes; save it because it contains valuable vitamins and minerals that will add flavour and goodness to soups, gravies and sauces.

Soups

What could be more inviting than a bowl of steaming soup and a cosy log fire on a raw winter evening? Hot soup is an old-fashioned defroster that never fails to work, and it can be made using odds and ends from the fridge and vegetable rack at little cost, and then frozen for a rainy day. Potatoes are especially good in soups because the starch in them thickens and enriches the soup, so you don't need to add flour, and the potatoes also add vitamins, a little protein and fibre, and, of course, flavour.

For chilly picnics or outings, take hot soup in a wide-necked thermos flask, with crispy wholewheat bread rolls and cheese, and maybe a quiche and some fruit. Curried Potato and Parsnip Soup is a favourite warmer for frozen spectators during rugby matches, and for a main course soup, try Scallop Chowder or real Scotch Broth. Chicken and Gnocchi Soup is delicately flavoured yet substantial, and seems to work wonders when you are recovering from the 'flu!

Scotch Broth

25 g/1 oz pearl barley, washed
275 g/10 oz scrag end or middle neck of lamb or mutton
1.4 litres/2½ pints chicken stock or water
1 onion, diced
25 g/1 oz yellow split peas
2 carrots, diced
2 leeks, sliced
¼ swede, diced
2 potatoes, diced
salt and pepper
1 tablespoon chopped parsley

Put the barley and lamb into a large saucepan and cover with fresh water. Bring slowly to the boil, then drain off the water, rinse out the pan and return the meat and barley to the pan. Add the chicken stock or water, onion, split peas, carrot, leek and swede. Cover the pan, bring to the boil and simmer gently until the meat is tender – about 1½ hours.

Lift out the lamb and dice the meat, discarding the bones and gristle. Return the meat to the pan and add the potato and salt and pepper to taste. Simmer for a further 20 minutes. Add the parsley and serve the broth in hot soup bowls. *Serves 6*

Chicken and Gnocchi Soup

2 chicken portions
900 ml/1½ pints chicken stock or water
1 large onion, halved
2 sticks celery, sliced
1 carrot, sliced
bay leaf
small slice of root ginger
salt and pepper
Gnocchi
450 g/1 lb potatoes, scrubbed
50 g/2 oz butter
1 egg
1 egg yolk
65 g/2½ oz flour
salt and pepper
grated nutmeg

First make the gnocchi. Set the oven at moderately hot (190 C, 375 F, gas 5). Prick the potatoes, place them on a baking tray or in a roasting tin and bake in the heated oven for 1 to 1½ hours, until tender. Cool the potatoes slightly, peel them and push the potato thugh a sieve or mash it until very smooth. Beat in the butter, whole egg, egg yolk and flour. Season to taste with salt, pepper and grated nutmeg. Set aside while you make the soup.

Trim off any excess fat from the chicken portions and put them into a saucepan with the stock or water. Singe the cut surfaces of the onion over a gas flame or on an electric plate until almost black, then add the onion halves to the pan – they will add colour to the soup. Add also the celery, carrot, bay leaf, root ginger and a little salt and pepper. Cover, bring to the boil and simmer for 30 minutes, or until the chicken is tender. Remove the chicken portions from the pan and continue to simmer the soup, uncovered, for a further 30 minutes.

Strain the soup and discard the vegetables, bay leaf and ginger. Skin and bone the chicken portions and dice the meat.

Return the meat to the pan with the strained soup. Bring to the boil, then reduce to a simmer. Poach teaspoonfuls of the gnocchi mixture in the soup, in several batches, for 5 minutes each. When all the gnocchi mixture has been used, taste the soup for seasoning. Then return all the gnocchi to the pan, bring the soup to the boil and serve immediately. *Serves 6*

Hungarian Potato Soup

(Illustrated on page 41)

25 g/1 oz butter
1 large onion, finely chopped
1 teaspoon medium-hot paprika
225 g/8 oz lean steak, finely diced
1 (397-g/14-oz) can chopped tomatoes
1 red pepper, deseeded and diced
1 large potato, peeled and diced
1 clove garlic, crushed
900 ml/1½ pints beef stock
salt and pepper
1 (142-ml/5-fl oz) carton soured cream

Melt the butter in a heavy saucepan, add the onion and cook gently until soft but not browned. Stir in the paprika and steak and cook over medium-high heat, stirring constantly, for 1 minute. Add the tomato, red pepper, potato, garlic, stock and a little salt. Cover and simmer gently until the meat is tender; the length of time this takes will depend upon the cut of meat used. Taste the soup and season with salt and pepper. Serve immediately, with the soured cream handed separately, and with crusty bread. *Serves 4*

Soissons Soup

25 g/1 oz butter
100 g/4 oz bacon, gammon or ham, diced
1 large onion, sliced
2 leeks, sliced
50 g/2 oz dried white haricot beans, soaked and
drained
1 or 2 cloves garlic, crushed
1.15 litres/2 pints chicken stock or water
bouquet garni · 1 potato, diced
50 g/2 oz French beans, cut into 5-mm/$\frac{1}{4}$-in pieces
salt and pepper

Melt the butter in a saucepan, add the bacon, gammon or ham, and the onion and leek. Cook slowly, stirring occasionally, until the onion and leek are soft but not browned. Add the beans, garlic, stock or water and bouquet garni, cover the pan and bring to the boil. Simmer gently for 1 hour, or until the beans are almost tender.

Add the potato and beans to the pan and season to taste. Simmer for a further 20 minutes, then remove the bouquet garni and serve immediately. This soup is especially good sprinkled with grated Parmesan cheese. *Serves 4*

Sweet Corn and Potato Chowder

(Illustrated on page 41)

25 g/1 oz butter
100 g/4 oz rindless streaky bacon, diced
3 large potatoes, peeled and diced
1 large onion, chopped
1 (425-g/15-oz) can cream-style sweet corn
750 ml/1¼ pints chicken stock
100 g/4 oz cooked smoked haddock, skinned, boned
and flaked
150 ml/¼ pint single cream
1 tablespoon chopped parsley
salt and pepper

Melt the butter in a large saucepan, add the bacon and fry over a medium-high heat until golden. Add the potato and onion, cover the pan, reduce the heat and cook slowly until the onion is soft but not browned. Add the sweet corn, stock and fish and simmer gently for 10 to 15 minutes. Stir in the cream and chopped parsley and season to taste with salt and pepper. *Serves 4*

Variation

Scallop Chowder

Substitute 225 g/8 oz of sliced cleaned scallops for the smoked haddock, adding them to the pan with the potato and onion.

Thick Vegetable Soup

This is a favourite soup in my family. My mother freezes reduced chicken stock in ice-cube trays to add extra flavour to the soup.

2 potatoes
2 carrots
2 onions
2 leeks
1 turnip
1 swede
1 parsnip
100 g/4 oz Jerusalem artichokes (optional)
3 sticks celery
about 1.15 litres/2 pints chicken stock or water
salt and pepper
1 tablespoon chopped parsley

Peel and dice all the vegetables except for the celery, which should be washed and sliced. Put all the vegetables into a large saucepan with 1.15 litres/2 pints of stock or water. Cover the pan, bring to the boil and simmer gently for 30 minutes, or until the vegetables are soft. Cool slightly, then press the soup through a sieve or purée it in a blender. Return the soup to the pan and add a little more liquid if necessary, to make a fairly thick soup. Reheat and season to taste with salt and pepper. Serve the soup, sprinkled with parsley, in warmed soup bowls, accompanied by crusty bread. *Serves 6*

Cream of Spinach Soup

50 g /2 oz butter
2 onions, sliced
2 potatoes, peeled and diced
1 (227-g /8-oz) packet frozen chopped spinach
900 ml/ 1½ pints chicken stock
salt and pepper
grated nutmeg
150 ml/¼ pint single cream
1 egg yolk (optional)
Croûtons
3 thickly cut slices bread, cut into small dice
4 tablespoons oil

Melt the butter in a saucepan. Add the onion and cook slowly until soft but not browned. Add the potato, spinach and stock. Bring to the boil, then reduce the heat and simmer gently for 20 minutes. Cool slightly, then press the soup through a sieve or purée it in a blender. Strain the soup and return it to the pan. Season to taste with salt, pepper and grated nutmeg and bring back to the boil.

Meanwhile, mix the cream with the egg yolk, if using. To make the croûtons, fry the diced bread in the oil in a frying pan, until golden brown and crisp. Drain the croûtons on absorbent kitchen paper and sprinkle them with salt. Remove the soup from the heat and stir in the cream. Serve immediately, with the croûtons. *Serves 6*

Variation
Watercress Soup

(Illustrated on page 41)

Replace the spinach with 225 g /8 oz chopped watercress sprigs.

Vichyssoise

50 g/2 oz butter
1 onion, finely chopped
450 g/1 lb leeks, sliced
3 sticks celery, sliced
450 g/1 lb potatoes, peeled and diced
600 ml/1 pint chicken stock
600 ml/1 pint hot milk
salt and pepper
150 ml/$\frac{1}{4}$ pint single cream
1 tablespoon chopped fresh herbs (chives, parsley, celery leaves)

Melt the butter in a large saucepan. Add the onion, leek and celery and cook gently, stirring occasionally, until soft. Stir in the potato, stock and milk and bring to the boil. Cover the pan and simmer gently for 15 to 20 minutes, or until the potato is tender. Remove the pan from the heat. Press the soup through a sieve or purée it in a blender, then strain. Season to taste with salt and pepper and allow to cool completely. Chill for as long as possible, preferably overnight. To serve, stir in the cream and sprinkle on the herbs. Spoon the soup into chilled bowls and serve with Melba toast (see below). If liked, vichyssoise can also be served hot. *Serves 4*

Variation

To make a hearty leek and potato soup, follow the recipe above but do not purée the soup, and serve it hot, without the cream.

Melba Toast

(Illustrated on page 41)

Toast medium-sliced white bread under a grill until brown on both sides. Remove from the grill and, working as quickly as possible, cut off the crusts and slice horizontally through each piece of bread to form two very thin slices. Place the thin slices under the grill for a few minutes, until they have curled at the edges and are crisp and brown.

Curried Potato and Parsnip Soup

25 g / 1 oz butter
1 onion, chopped
2 teaspoons curry powder, or to taste
1 potato, peeled and sliced
450 g / 1 lb parsnips, sliced
900 ml / 1½ pints chicken stock or water
salt and pepper
1 tablespoon chopped parsley or coriander leaves

Melt the butter in a saucepan, add the onion and cook slowly until soft but not browned. Stir in the curry powder and cook for 2 minutes, stirring constantly. Stir in the potato and parsnip. Cook for 1 minute, stirring constantly. Pour on the stock or water and add a little salt and pepper. Cover the pan, bring to the boil and simmer gently for 15 to 20 minutes, until the vegetables are soft.

Cool the soup slightly then press it through a sieve or purée it in a blender. Return the soup to the pan, reheat and adjust the seasoning to taste. Sprinkle with the parsley or coriander leaves before serving. *Serves 4*

Starters and Snacks

It's often difficult to find easy yet unusual and inexpensive ways to start a meal. Don't give up! The versatile potato can be used for a range of starters from Spinach and Cheese Soufflé to Taramasalata. And as nibbles with drinks, serve 'Cheese' Straws; they taste very cheesy, yet, incredibly, there isn't any cheese in the recipe.

Commercially prepared, ready-to-eat snacks may be quick but they are generally expensive and are often of little nutritional value compared with a snack prepared at home. Savoury Pumpkin Pie does take a little time to prepare but, once cooked, it can be cut into individual portions, wrapped separately and frozen. Then it only takes a few minutes in a hot oven to thaw and heat through a slice of the pie, as and when you need it.

Savoury Pumpkin Pie

450 g/1 lb pumpkin
salt and pepper
50 g/2 oz butter
1 large onion, sliced
350 g/12 oz potatoes, scrubbed
1 (368-g/13-oz) packet frozen puff pastry
1 egg, beaten

Peel the pumpkin and cut the flesh into cubes, discarding the seeds. Put the pumpkin cubes into a saucepan with water to cover and add a large pinch of salt. Bring to the boil, then reduce the heat and cook gently until soft – about 15 minutes. Drain very thoroughly then return to the pan. Meanwhile, melt the butter in a frying pan, add the onion and cook gently until soft and golden brown. Add to the pumpkin, stirring well to mix. Put the potatoes into a pan with cold, salted water to cover. Bring to the boil and simmer gently until the potatoes are almost tender. Drain them and allow to cool slightly. Peel the potatoes and cut them into 1-cm/½-in dice. Stir the diced potato into the pumpkin mixture, with salt and pepper to taste.

Roll the pastry out thinly and cut out two circles – one 25 cm/10 in. in diameter, the other 30 cm/12 in. in diameter. Place the smaller circle on a greased baking sheet. Spread the pumpkin filling over the pastry, leaving a 1-cm/½-in border of pastry round the outside of the circle and mounding the filling in the centre. Brush the pastry border with beaten egg, then place the second circle of pastry on top. Press well to seal and scallop the edges with a knife. Any remaining scraps of pastry can be cut into shapes to décorate the top.

Set the oven at hot (220 C, 425F, gas 7). Chill the pie for 15 minutes, then brush it with beaten egg. Bake the pie in the heated oven for 15 minutes, then reduce the heat to moderately hot (190 C, 375F, gas 5) and bake for a further 15 minutes, until the pastry is crisp and brown. Transfer to a serving plate, cut into wedges and serve hot. *Serves 6–8*

Potato Puffs
with Red Pepper Sauce

(Illustrated on page 42)

450 g/1 lb potatoes, peeled
salt and pepper
15 g/½ oz butter
40 g/1½ oz plain flour
1 egg, beaten
50 g/2 oz Cheddar cheese, finely diced
oil for deep frying
Red Pepper Sauce
2 red peppers
2 onions, chopped
2 cloves garlic
2 tablespoons coarsely chopped parsley
1 red chilli pepper, deseeded and chopped (optional)
150 ml/¼ pint white wine vinegar
50 g/2 oz soft brown sugar
salt

Cook the potatoes in boiling salted water until just soft. Drain them well, return to the empty pan and dry over low heat for 2 minutes. Push the potatoes through a sieve or mash them thoroughly. Put the butter and 4 tablespoons of water into a small pan, heat until the butter has melted then bring to the boil. Quickly tip in the flour and beat well until the mixture leaves the sides of the pan, then gradually beat in the egg. Beat this mixture into the mashed potato and season well. Stir in the cheese.

To make the sauce, grill the red peppers until the skins blister, then peel them. Remove the cores and seeds and chop the flesh roughly. Put it into a blender or food processor, with the onion, garlic, parsley, chilli pepper and vinegar, and blend until smooth. Put the purée into a pan with the sugar and bring slowly to the boil, stirring frequently. Boil over high heat, stirring constantly, for about 5 minutes, until the sauce is very thick Add salt to taste and keep warm.

Heat the oil to 190 C/375 F and carefully drop in teaspoonfuls of the potato mixture. Cook for about 2 minutes, until the puffs are crisp and golden. Remove with a slotted spoon and drain on absorbent kitchen paper. Serve at once, with the hot Red Pepper Sauce. *Serves 4*

Vegetable Gratin

For a vegetarian main dish, add six chopped hard-boiled eggs to the sauce when you add the cheese and vegetables.

15 g/½ oz butter
15 g/½ oz plain flour
300 ml/½ pint milk (or half milk and half vegetable cooking water)
100 g/4 oz grated cheese
450 g/1 lb lightly cooked vegetables (a selection from the following: whole small new potatoes or peeled and diced large potatoes, sliced courgettes, peas, quartered carrots, French beans, diced parsnips, Brussels sprouts, cauliflower florets, diced aubergine, whole okra, sweet corn kernels, strips of green and red pepper)
salt and pepper

Make a sauce by melting the butter in a saucepan, stirring in the flour, then gradually whisking in the milk (or milk and vegetable cooking water). Bring to the boil, whisking constantly, then reduce the heat and simmer gently for 2 minutes. Set the oven at hot (220 C, 425 F, gas 7). Remove the pan from the heat and stir in two-thirds of the cheese and all the vegetables. Season to taste with salt and pepper. Spoon the mixture into a greased ovenproof gratin dish, sprinkle with the remaining cheese and bake in the heated oven for 10 to 15 minutes, until brown and bubbling. Serve immediately. *Serves 4*

Taramasalata

(Illustrated on page 42)

450 g/1 lb potatoes, peeled, boiled, cooled and grated
1 Spanish onion, grated
1 (200-g/7.05-oz) jar cod's roe
about 150 ml/¼ pint oil
lemon juice
2 cloves garlic, crushed (optional)
salt and pepper
pieces of green pepper to garnish

Put the grated potato and onion into the bowl of an electric mixer or food processsor or into a large mixing bowl. Mash the cod's roe with a fork then gradually add it to the potato, beating well. When the mixture is smooth, gradually beat in the oil, lemon juice to taste, and the garlic if using. Beat the mixture until it is white and tastes balanced, then season to taste. Spoon the taramasalata into a bowl, garnish with pieces of green pepper, and chill before serving. *Serves 6*

Cheese and Spinach Soufflé

225 g/8 oz mashed potato
1 (227-g/8-oz) packet frozen chopped spinach
15 g/½ oz butter
100 g/4 oz grated cheese
4 eggs, separated
salt and pepper · grated nutmeg

Beat the mashed potato until very smooth. Put the spinach in a saucepan with the butter and cook slowly until completely thawed. Increase the heat and boil to evaporate any liquid.

When the spinach is dry add it to the mashed potato, with two-thirds of the grated cheese. Beat until smooth, then stir in the egg yolks. Season well with salt, pepper and grated nutmeg.

Set the oven at moderately hot (190 C, 375F, gas 5). Grease a 1.15-litre/2-pint soufflé dish. Whisk the egg whites until very stiff, then stir a little into the potato mixture. Carefully fold in the remaining egg white. Spoon the mixture into the prepared soufflé dish and sprinkle with the remaining cheese. Cook in the heated oven for 25 to 30 minutes, until puffed and browned. Serve immediately. *Serves 6*

Variations

Cheese and Sweet Corn Soufflé

Replace the spinach with 1 (198-g/7-oz) can of sweet corn, drained. There is no need to heat the corn; just stir it into the mashed potato with the cheese, then continue as above.

Crab Soufflé

Replace the spinach with 1 (169-g/6-oz) can of crabmeat, drained and flaked. Stir the crabmeat into the mashed potato with the cheese.

Potato Nests
with Seafood Filling

(Illustrated on page 42)

450 g/1 lb potatoes, peeled
salt and pepper
1 egg yolk
about 3 tablespoons hot milk
grated nutmeg
25 g/1 oz butter, melted
chopped parsley and unpeeled prawns to garnish
Seafood Filling
15 g/½ oz butter
15 g/½ oz plain flour
150 ml/¼ pint milk
150 ml/¼ pint single cream
225 g/8 oz mixed seafood (a combination of crabmeat,
shrimps, prawns, scallops and mussels)
salt and pepper
few drops lemon juice (optional)

Put the potatoes in a pan of salted water. Cover the pan and bring to the boil. Reduce the heat and simmer until the potatoes are tender – 20 to 25 minutes, depending on size and variety. Drain them thoroughly, then push them through a sieve or mash until very smooth. Beat in the egg yolk and enough hot milk to make a purée that can be piped – it should not be too soft. Season with salt, pepper and grated nutmeg and leave to cool.

When the mixture is cool enough to handle, use it to fill a piping bag fitted with a large star nozzle. Pipe four nests, each about 7.5 cm/3 in. in diameter, on to a greased ovenproof dish. Set the oven at hot (220 C, 425 F, gas 7). Brush the nests with the melted butter and bake them in the oven for 10 to 15 minutes, until lightly browned.

To make the filling, melt the butter in a saucepan, stir in the flour and gradually whisk in the milk and cream. Bring to the boil, whisking constantly, and simmer gently for 1 minute. Add

28

any uncooked seafood, such as scallops, and simmer gently for 2 to 3 minutes. (Raw mussels should first be steamed until the shells open and the mussels can be removed. Any mussels that are cracked or broken, or that do not open after being cooked, should be discarded.) Finally, add the crabmeat and peeled shrimps and prawns. Simmer gently until thoroughly heated. Season to taste, adding a few drops of lemon juice if desired.

Fill the potato nests with the seafood filling and sprinkle on some chopped parsley. Arrange a few unpeeled prawns round the base and serve immediately. *Serves 4*

'Cheese' Straws

Although these 'cheese' straws contain no cheese, they taste very cheesy!

75 g /3 oz butter
75 g /3 oz plain flour
75 g /3 oz cold cooked potato, grated
water, milk or beaten egg to glaze
sea salt
caraway seeds

Mix together the butter, flour and grated potato and knead to form a dough. Wrap the dough and chill it for 30 minutes in the refrigerator.

Set the oven at moderately hot (190 C, 375 F, gas 5). Roll out the dough fairly thinly on a floured board. Brush the dough with glaze and sprinkle with salt and caraway seeds. Using a sharp knife or a pastry wheel, cut the dough into strips measuring 6×1 cm/$2\frac{1}{2} \times \frac{1}{2}$ in. Transfer the strips to a greased baking tray and bake in the heated oven for 10 minutes. Cool on a wire rack. *Makes 40–50*

Spicy Potato Balls in Curry Sauce

350 g / 12 oz mashed potato
40 g / 1½ oz plain flour
½ green pepper, deseeded and finely chopped
small piece of fresh root ginger, finely grated
pinch of ground coriander
salt
oil for deep frying
Curry Sauce
1 tablespoon oil
1 large onion, finely chopped
1 clove garlic, crushed
2 teaspoons curry powder, or to taste
1 (397-g / 14-oz) can chopped tomatoes
salt and pepper
1 tablespoon mango chutney
1 tablespoon tomato purée

Mix the potato with the flour, green pepper, root ginger, coriander, and salt to taste. Using floured hands, shape the mixture into walnut-sized balls. Heat the oil to 190 C/375 F and deep fry the potato balls, a few at a time, for 3 to 4 minutes, until they are crisp and golden. Drain on absorbent kitchen paper.

Meanwhile, make the sauce. Heat the oil and gently cook the onion until soft. Add the garlic and curry powder, cook for 1 minute, stirring, then add the chopped tomatoes, tomato purée and chutney. Simmer for about 10 minutes. Season to taste and serve, with the hot potato balls. *Serves 4*

Main Dishes

If you love good quality meat for main meals, but a visit to the butchers means taking out a mortgage to cover the high cost, then this chapter will come to the aid of your purse! Potatoes can make meat, fish and poultry go further than you had imagined, without sacrificing goodness, quality, taste or too much time. For fans of Chinese food there is a recipe for Cantonese Puffs – vegetables and meat in a crisp batter with a mouth-watering sauce. And for those extra special meals – celebrations, bank holidays and dinner parties – there are half a dozen or so ritzy recipes at the end of the chapter, such as Guiness-braised Steaks with Fondant Potatoes – a luxurious version of steak and chips. And if you like to cook meals without meat try the Vegetable Curry or the Soufflé-topped Vegetable Casserole. Potatoes make a square meal!

Traditional Shepherd's Pie

The best shepherd's pie is made from cold roast lamb, usually left over from Sunday lunch, and cottage pie is traditionally made in the same way, using leftover roast beef. However, minced raw lamb or beef can make a pie just as good, provided the meat used is freshly minced and is good quality lean meat; cheap, fatty mince is always a false economy. Whichever type of meat you use, it must be highly seasoned and very tasty – bland shepherd's pie is horrible!

3 tablespoons oil
2 large onions, chopped
450 g/1 lb cooked or raw lean lamb or beef, minced
1 or 2 tablespoons flour
300 ml/$\frac{1}{2}$ pint leftover gravy or good meat stock
1 tablespoon Worcestershire sauce
3 tablespoons tomato ketchup
salt and pepper
Topping
675 g/1$\frac{1}{2}$ lb potatoes, peeled
salt and pepper
4 tablespoons hot milk
50 g/2 oz butter
grated nutmeg

Heat the oil in a heavy pan and add the onions. Stir well, cover and cook over low heat until the onions are very soft and transparent – 10 to 15 minutes. Add the meat. Fry over a high heat – 1 minute for cooked meat and about 5 minutes for raw – until the meat has broken up and is a good brown colour all over; it should not be grey. Add the flour – use 1 tablespoon if you are using gravy and 2 tablespoons if you are using stock. Stir well and cook for 1 minute, then stir in the gravy or stock, and the Worcestershire sauce and ketchup. Bring to the boil and simmer for 5 minutes if using cooked meat, and for 45 minutes if using raw meat. Add salt and pepper to taste. Stir well then tip the meat mixture into a greased ovenproof baking dish.

While the meat is simmering, make the topping. Cook the potatoes in boiling salted water until tender, then drain thoroughly and press through a sieve or mash until smooth. Beat in the hot milk and butter and season to taste with salt, pepper and grated nutmeg. Set the oven at moderately hot (190 C, 375F, gas 5).

Pipe or spread the mashed potato over the meat in the baking dish. Place in the heated oven for 30 to 40 minutes, until the pie is golden brown and bubbling. *Serves 4*

Variations

1. Add a couple of diced cooked carrots to the meat mixture before baking.

2. Sprinkle 75 g/3 oz of grated cheese over the potato topping before baking.

3. Add a few tablespoons of cooked red kidney beans to the meat mixture before baking.

Cornish Pasties

225 g/8 oz plain flour (white or wholemeal)
50 g/2 oz lard or white vegetable fat
50 g/2 oz butter
generous pinch of salt
1 egg, beaten
Filling
225 g/8 oz lean beef, finely diced
1 small onion, finely chopped
1 potato, peeled and finely diced
1 small turnip, finely diced
1 tablespoon chopped parsley
salt and pepper

Set the oven at hot (220 C, 425F, gas 7). Put the flour into a mixing bowl. Cut the fats into small pieces and add to the bowl. Using the tips of your fingers, rub the fats into the flour until the mixture resembles fine breadcrumbs. Mix the salt with 4 tablespoons cold water and add to the flour mixture, mixing to form a soft but not sticky dough. Roll out the dough 5 mm/$\frac{1}{4}$ in thick, then cut out four 15-cm/6-in circles.

To make the filling, mix the beef with the onion, potato, turnip, parsley and a little salt and pepper. Divide the filling between the four pastry circles. Brush the edges with water and bring them together above the filling. Press together firmly and flute the seam. Make a small steam hole in the top. Brush with beaten egg and place on a greased baking sheet.

Bake the pasties in the heated oven for 15 minutes, then reduce the oven temperature to moderate (180 C, 350F, gas 4) and bake for a further 30 minutes. Serve, hot or cold, with salad.
Makes 4

Variations

Curried Lamb Pasties

Follow the recipe for Cornish Pasties (left), using the following filling instead:

225 g/8 oz lean lamb, diced
1 small onion, finely chopped
1 potato, peeled and diced
25 g/1 oz dried apricots, soaked, drained and chopped
1 tablespoon raisins
1 tablespoon chopped almonds
2 tablespoons hot mango chutney
salt and pepper
curry powder

Mix all the filling ingredients together, seasoning to taste with salt, pepper and curry powder.

Rough Puff Pastry

For a change try making pasties with rough puff pastry instead of shortcrust. Use the pastry ingredients as for Cornish Pasties (left) but use the following method.

Put the flour and salt into a mixing bowl. Make sure the fats are well chilled, then cut them into small flakes the size of a thumbnail. Add them to the bowl and stir with a knife to coat with flour. Mix in 4 tablespoons cold water, using a knife. The mixture should hold together but look lumpy – totally unlike shortcrust pastry.

Turn the dough out on to a floured work surface and roll it out into a 30 × 10-cm/12 × 4-in rectangle. Fold the bottom third of the dough up to cover the middle third, then fold the top third of the dough down to make a kind of envelope or sandwich; this folding method is called a 'turn'. You should now have a 10-cm/4-in square of dough. Wrap the dough in greaseproof paper or cling film and chill for 15 minutes. Roll out the dough as before, do another turn and chill. Then roll out and fold for a third time. The dough is now ready to use.

Farmhouse Casserole

675 g/1½ lb potatoes, peeled
225 g/8 oz swede
25 g/1 oz plain flour
salt and pepper
450 g/1 lb stewing steak
1 small onion, sliced
600 ml/1 pint beef stock
25 g/1 oz butter

Set the oven at moderate (160 C, 325F, gas 3). Slice two of the potatoes and cut the remainder, with the swede, into small cubes. Season the flour with salt and pepper. Cut the meat into 2.5-cm/1-in cubes and toss them in the seasoned flour. Put the meat, potato and swede cubes and the sliced onion into a large ovenproof casserole and arrange the slices of potato on top. Pour on the stock, dot the top with the butter and cover. Bake in the oven for 1½ hours, then increase the oven temperature to hot (220 C, 425F, gas 7), remove the lid of the casserole and cook for 20 to 30 minutes, until the potatoes are brown. *Serves 4–6*

Variations
Winter Casserole

Slice a Savoy cabbage into six wedges and place in a pan of boiling salted water. Simmer for 1 minute, then remove and drain thoroughly. Follow the recipe above, omitting the sliced potatoes – reduce the potato quantity to 350 g/12 oz. Add the cabbage to the casserole at the same time as the meat and vegetables and proceed as above. You'll need to use a large casserole for this recipe.

Steak and Kidney Casserole

Follow the recipe for Farmhouse Casserole, adding 100 g/4 oz of diced kidney to the meat before you toss it in seasoned flour. Use 2 onions instead of 1 and, for a really rich casserole, add 100 g/4 oz of button mushrooms.

Layered Pork and Potato Bake

4 rashers rindless streaky bacon, chopped
1 large onion, chopped
100 g/4 oz mushrooms, quartered
1 teaspoon chopped fresh sage or $\frac{1}{2}$ teaspoon dried
sage
1 teaspoon chopped fresh thyme or $\frac{1}{2}$ teaspoon dried
thyme
salt and pepper
450 g/1 lb lean pork, cubed
450 g/1 lb potatoes, peeled and sliced
300 ml/$\frac{1}{2}$ pint chicken stock
25 g/1 oz butter, cut into flakes

Gently fry the bacon in a frying pan for 3 minutes. Add the onion and cook gently until soft. Add the mushrooms, sage, thyme and seasoning and cook for a further minute. Then remove from the pan and set aside. Cook the pork cubes in the pan juices until browned, then mix them with the bacon mixture.

Put one-third of the mixture into the bottom of a casserole. Cover with a layer of potatoes. Add a second layer of the pork mixture, topped with a second layer of potatoes, then add a third layer of each. Pour the stock over the mixture. Put flakes of butter over the top layer of potatoes. Cover the casserole and bake in a moderate oven (180 C, 350F, gas 4) for $1\frac{1}{2}$ hours. Remove the lid and cook for a further 15 minutes, to brown the potatoes. *Serves 4–6*

Cheshire Pie

450 g/1 lb lean pork from the leg or fillet, cut into
2.5-cm/1-in cubes
1 tablespoon flour
2 tablespoons oil
1 large cooking apple, peeled, cored and sliced
1 large potato, peeled and thinly sliced
1 onion, thinly sliced
salt and pepper
150 ml/$\frac{1}{4}$ pint cider
1 (212-g/7$\frac{1}{2}$-oz) packet frozen puff pastry, thawed
1 egg, beaten

Set the oven at hot (220 C, 425F, gas 7). Toss the pork cubes in
the flour. Heat the oil in a frying pan and quickly brown the pork
on all sides. Layer the pork with the apple, potato and onion
slices in a pie dish, seasoning lightly between each layer. Pour
over the cider.

Roll out the pastry into an oval slightly larger than the pie
dish. Cut a narrow strip from the edge of the pastry and press
the strip on to the rim of the pie dish, moistening the rim first.
Brush this pastry rim with beaten egg, then cover the pie with
the pastry oval. Press the edges down firmly to seal. Decorate
the pie with pastry trimmings and make a small hole in the top
for the steam to escape.

Brush the pie with beaten egg and bake it in the heated oven
for 15 minutes, until browned. Then cover the pie with dam-
pened greaseproof paper or foil, lower the oven temperature
to moderate (160 C, 325F, gas 3) and bake for a further 45
minutes. *Serves 4*

Sausage Goulash

(Illustrated on page 59)

This Hungarian dish is traditionally made with frankfurters but I think it is even better made with 'home-made' sausages from the butchers, or supermarket sausages that have extra herbs and spices.

2 tablespoons oil
675 g/1½ lb sausages or frankfurters
4 large onions, sliced
1 tablespoon paprika, or to taste
1 tablespoon flour
1 tablespoon tomato purée
1 (397-g/14-oz) can tomatoes
1 (397-g/14-oz) can chopped tomatoes
1 teaspoon Bovril · salt and pepper
450 g/1 lb small new potatoes, scraped
3 tablespoons natural yogurt or soured cream

Put the oil and sausages or frankfurters into a flameproof casserole. Heat gently, to prevent the skins bursting, then quickly brown; you may need to do this in two batches. Remove from the casserole and set aside. Add the onions to the fat in the casserole, cover and cook slowly until soft – about 15 minutes. Then remove the lid, increase the heat and allow the onions to brown. Stir in the paprika and stir-fry for 1 minute over low heat. Stir in the flour and tomato purée, followed by the whole and chopped tomatoes and their juice. Bring to the boil, stirring constantly, then stir in the Bovril and add salt and pepper to taste. Cut each sausage or frankfurter into two or three pieces, depending on size, and stir into the casserole with the potatoes.

Cover the casserole and simmer gently for 20 to 25 minutes, until the potatoes are tender. If the sauce is a bit thin, remove the lid for the last 10 minutes of cooking time. Taste for seasoning, then add the yogurt or soured cream, stirring two or three times to give a marbled effect, if liked. *Serves 4–6*

Puchero

2 tablespoons oil
150 g/6 oz lean stewing steak, cubed
150 g/6 oz lean pork, cubed
1 large onion, chopped
1 clove garlic, crushed
2 tablespoons flour
225 g/8 oz dried chick peas, soaked and drained
1 (425-g/15-oz) can tomatoes
900 ml/1½ pints beef stock
1 (425-g/15 oz) can borlotti beans, drained
3 large potatoes, peeled and cubed
100 g/4 oz French beans, cut into 2.5-cm/1-in lengths
salt and pepper

Heat the oil in a frying pan, add the beef and pork and fry until browned on all sides, then remove. Stir the onion and garlic into the frying pan and cook until soft, then sprinkle on the flour and fry briefly, stirring. Transfer the onion and garlic and browned meat to a large saucepan. Add the chick peas, tomatoes and stock and bring to the boil. Reduce the heat, cover the pan and simmer for 1 to 1½ hours, or until the meat is tender. Add the borlotti beans, potatoes, French beans and seasoning to taste, and simmer for a further 40 minutes. *Serves 6*

From the top: *Melba Toast (page 20); Hungarian Potato Soup (page 15); Sweet Corn and Potato Chowder (page 17); Watercress Soup (page 19)*

Lamb Korma

675 g/1½ lb lean lamb from the leg or shoulder, cubed
3 large onions, thinly sliced
3 cloves garlic, crushed
bay leaf
1 teaspoon chilli powder, or to taste
½ teaspoon salt
½ teaspoon ground turmeric
pinch of ground cloves
5-cm/2-in piece root ginger, peeled and chopped
½ teaspoon ground coriander
750 ml/1¼ pints whole milk natural yogurt
1 tablespoon oil
4 large potatoes, peeled and quartered

Put the lamb cubes into a glass or china bowl with the onions, garlic and bay leaf. Mix together the chilli powder, salt, turmeric, cloves, ginger, coriander and yogurt, and spoon over the meat. Stir well, then cover and leave to marinate in the refrigerator overnight.

The next day, stir the meat and marinade well. Set the oven at moderately hot (190 C, 375F, gas 5). Heat the oil in a heavy flameproof casserole, add the meat and the marinade and stir in the potatoes. Then cover the casserole and cook for about 1½ hours, until the meat and potatoes are tender. During cooking the sauce will separate out. Stir well and serve with boiled brown rice, tomato salad and chutney. If you prefer a smooth sauce, remove the meat and potatoes after cooking and purée the onions and sauce in a blender until smooth. *Serves 4*

From the top: *Potato Nest with Seafood Filling (page 28); Potato Puffs with Red Pepper Sauce (page 24); Taramasalata (page 26)*

Fillets of Fish Chauchat

The great French chef Escoffier, who was called 'the king of chefs and the chef of kings', invented this recipe with the everyday cook in mind. Almost any type of white fish can be used – sole fillets are the most luxurious but expensive; haddock, cod, whiting and plaice all make good substitutes.

4 (100 to 150-g/4 to 5-oz) fillets of white fish, skinned
300 ml/½ pint milk
bay leaf
few peppercorns
1 slice onion
450 g/1 lb medium-sized new potatoes
salt and pepper
75 g/3 oz butter
1 tablespoon flour
3–4 tablespoons single or double cream
50 g/2 oz grated Parmesan cheese

Set the oven at moderate (180 C, 350 F, gas 4). Rinse the fish fillets, pat them dry, fold them in half and place them in a greased ovenproof baking dish. Pour over the milk and add the bay leaf, peppercorns and slice of onion, slipping them down the sides of the dish, below the surface of the milk. Cover the dish with a lid or foil and cook in the heated oven for 15 to 20 minutes, until the fish flakes easily with a fork. Meanwhile, scrape the potatoes and cook them in boiling salted water until tender. Rinse them with cold water and allow to cool slightly, then slice them into rounds.

Melt 25 g/1 oz of the butter in a small pan and stir in the flour. Cook for a few seconds and remove from the heat. Strain the cooking liquid from the fish and whisk it into the flour mixture. Bring to the boil, whisking constantly to make a smooth sauce. Simmer for 2 minutes, then stir in the cream. Remove from the heat and stir in the remaining butter and the cheese. Season.

Spoon about one-third of the sauce into a greased ovenproof serving dish. Arrange the cooked fish fillets down the centre of the dish and surround the fish with potato slices. Spoon over the remaining sauce and place under a hot grill, or in a very hot oven (240 C, 475F, gas 9), until browned. *Serves 4*

Salmon Salad Loaf

(Illustrated on page 59)

225 g/8 oz new potatoes, scraped
salt and pepper
1 (213-g/7½-oz) can salmon
100 g/4 oz peeled cooked prawns
75 g/3 oz cucumber, diced
1 hard-boiled egg, chopped
1 tablespoon chopped chives or parsley
25 g/1 oz fresh white breadcrumbs
150 ml/¼ pint mayonnaise
cucumber slices and lettuce leaves to garnish

Lightly oil a 1-kg/2-lb loaf tin and line the base of the tin with greaseproof paper. Cook the potatoes in boiling salted water until tender. Drain the potatoes, dice them and leave to cool.

Flake the salmon and mix it with the prawns, diced cucumber, hard-boiled egg, herbs, breadcrumbs, mayonnaise and the cooled potatoes. Season to taste. Spoon the mixture into the prepared tin and press it down firmly with the back of a spoon. Chill overnight, or until firm. Turn out on to a plate and garnish with cucumber slices and lettuce leaves. *Serves 6*

Cantonese Puffs

450 g/1 lb potatoes, peeled
salt and pepper
25 g/1 oz butter
75 g/3 oz plain flour
3 eggs, beaten
oil for deep frying
100 g/4 oz button mushrooms
1 small cauliflower, broken into small florets
2 boned chicken breasts, cut into small dice
few spring onions to garnish
Sauce
1 (425-g/15-oz) can pineapple chunks in natural juice
4 tablespoons tomato ketchup
4 tablespoons soy sauce
2 tablespoons wine vinegar
1 tablespoon brown sugar, or to taste
4 teaspoons cornflour

Cook the potatoes in boiling salted water until tender. Drain thoroughly, then return to the pan and dry over low heat for a couple of minutes. Mash or sieve the potatoes. Put the butter and 300 ml/½ pint of water into a pan. Heat until the butter melts, then bring quickly to the boil. Tip in the flour immediately and beat well until the mixture leaves the sides of the pan. Beat in the eggs, followed by the mashed potato.

To make the sauce, heat the pineapple chunks with their juice and 300 ml/½ pint of water in a small pan. Mix the ketchup, soy sauce, vinegar, sugar and cornflour together in a small bowl. Stir in a little of the hot liquid, then return the whole mixture to the pan and bring to the boil, stirring. Simmer for 1 minute and adjust the seasoning to taste.

Heat the oil to 185C/360F. Coat the mushrooms, cauliflower and diced chicken in the potato batter. Fry in the heated oil until puffed and browned. Drain on absorbent kitchen paper, transfer to a dish and spoon over the sauce. Garnish with spring onion curls (spring onions shredded at both ends and soaked in iced water to curl). Serve with brown rice. *Serves 4*

Soufflé-topped Vegetable Casserole

4 large carrots, thickly sliced
3 large potatoes, peeled and cut into 1-cm/½-in dice
1 small turnip, cut into 1-cm/½-in dice
1 large onion, chopped
salt and pepper
8 tomatoes, peeled and deseeded
25 g/1 oz butter
25 g/1 oz plain flour
½ teaspoon mustard powder
300 ml/½ pint milk
3 eggs, separated
100 g/4 oz Cheddar cheese, grated
1 tablespoon chopped parsley

Cook the carrots, potatoes, turnip and onion in boiling salted water for 15 minutes. Drain and season to taste, then place in a 1.75-litre/3-pint ovenproof soufflé dish. Blend the tomatoes with a little seasoning until smooth and pour over the vegetable mixture.

Melt the butter in a pan, stir in the flour and mustard powder and cook for 1 minute, until smooth. Gradually stir in the milk, to make a smooth sauce. Allow it to cool slightly, then beat in the egg yolks and cheese. Whisk the egg whites until stiff and fold into the sauce. Pour the sauce over the vegetables in the soufflé dish. Bake in a moderately hot oven (190C, 375F, gas 5) until well risen and golden brown – about 40 minutes. Garnish with the chopped parsley before serving. *Serves 4*

Chicken and Pepper Gougère

450 g / 1 lb potatoes, peeled
salt
15 g/$\frac{1}{2}$ oz butter
40 g / 1$\frac{1}{2}$ oz flour
1 egg, beaten
50 g /2 oz Stilton, Gorgonzola or other blue cheese,
crumbled
Filling
25 g / 1 oz butter
1 small onion, finely chopped
20 g /$\frac{3}{4}$ oz flour
150 ml/$\frac{1}{4}$ pint chicken stock
150 ml/$\frac{1}{4}$ pint creamy milk
salt and pepper
450 g / 1 lb cooked chicken meat, cut into bite-sized
pieces
1 (184-g /6$\frac{1}{2}$-oz) can pimientos, drained and diced

Cook the potatoes in boiling salted water until tender. Drain very thoroughly, then return to the empty pan and dry over low heat for 1 to 2 minutes. Press the potatoes through a sieve or mash them thoroughly. Put the butter into a small pan with 4 tablespoons of water and a generous pinch of salt. Heat until the butter has melted, then bring to the boil. Quickly tip in the flour and beat well until the mixture leaves the sides of the pan. Gradually beat in the egg, then beat this mixture into the mashed potato, with the cheese. Thoroughly grease a large oval baking dish and place spoonfuls of the mixture round the outer edge of the dish. Set the oven at hot (220 C, 425F, gas 7).

To make the filling, cook the onion in the butter until soft. Stir in the flour, followed by the stock and milk. Stir until boiling, reduce the heat and simmer for 3 to 4 minutes. Season, then stir in the chicken and pimiento, and spoon into the gougère. Bake in the heated oven for 15 to 20 minutes, until crisp and golden.
Serves 4

Vegetable Curry

This dish makes a nutritious vegetarian main course, and it can also be served as an accompaniment to plainly roasted or grilled meats. If you can get fresh coriander leaves they add a wonderful flavour, chopped and sprinkled over the curry before serving.

1 aubergine, diced
salt and pepper
2 tablespoons oil
4 teaspoons mustard seeds
$\frac{1}{2}$ teaspoon ground turmeric
$1\frac{1}{2}$ teaspoons chilli powder
1 clove garlic, crushed
2.5-cm/1-in piece of root ginger, peeled and finely chopped
1 small cauliflower, broken into florets
3 potatoes, peeled and diced
4 courgettes, thickly sliced
4 tomatoes, peeled, quartered and deseeded
175 g/6 oz runner beans or French beans, cut into 2.5-cm/1-in lengths
100 g/4 oz shelled almonds, toasted

Sprinkle the diced aubergine with salt, allow to drain in a colander for ten minutes, then rinse and drain thoroughly; this process will remove any bitterness in the aubergine.

Heat the oil in a heavy flameproof casserole or in a large heavy frying pan with a lid. Add the mustard seeds, turmeric and chilli powder and cook, stirring constantly, until the seeds begin to pop. Stir in the garlic and ginger and fry for a few seconds. Then add all the vegetables to the casserole or pan, sprinkle with a little salt and stir thoroughly to blend all the spices and vegetables. Cover and cook very slowly for 40 to 50 minutes, until all the vegetables are tender. Taste for seasoning and stir in the almonds. *Serves 4*

Wholewheat Vegetable Pie

(Illustrated on page 59)

50 g/2 oz butter
25 g/1 oz lard or white vegetable fat
175 g/6 oz wholemeal flour
pinch of salt
25 g/1 oz grated Parmesan cheese
1 egg, beaten (optional)

Filling

2 large potatoes, peeled and diced
100 g/4 oz swede, diced
2 large carrots, diced
2 leeks, cut into 2.5-cm/1-in lengths
10 baby onions
salt and pepper
$\frac{1}{2}$ small cauliflower, broken into florets
100 g/4 oz frozen peas
1 small red pepper, deseeded and sliced
1 small green pepper, deseeded and sliced
3 tablespoons canned or frozen sweet corn
175 g/6 oz Edam cheese, diced
25 g/1 oz butter
25 g/1 oz wholewheat flour
150 ml/$\frac{1}{4}$ pint milk
chopped fresh herbs (optional)

First make the pastry. Rub the butter and lard or vegetable fat into the flour until the mixture resembles fine breadcrumbs. Stir in the salt, cheese and enough cold water to make a soft but not sticky dough. Wrap and chill.

Set the oven at moderately hot (190 C, 375F, gas 5). Put the potato, swede, carrot, leek and onions into a large saucepan and cover with cold water. Add a pinch of salt, then cover and bring to the boil. Simmer for 5 minutes, then add the cauliflower florets and peas. Simmer for a further 2 minutes, then drain and reserve the cooking liquid. Mix the cooked vegetables with the sliced peppers, sweet corn and cheese. Melt the butter in a pan, stir in the flour, then gradually stir in the milk and 150 ml/$\frac{1}{4}$ pint of the reserved cooking liquid. Bring to the boil, stirring constantly, and simmer for 3 minutes. Season to taste and stir in the herbs, if using. Mix with the vegetable and cheese mixture and spoon into a pie dish.

Roll out the pastry into an oval 5 cm/2 in larger than the pie dish. Cut a strip 1 cm/$\frac{1}{2}$ in wide from the edge of the pastry oval and brush it with beaten egg (if using) or with water. Press the strip, damp side down, on to the rim of the dish. Brush this pastry rim with more egg or water and cover the pie with the pastry oval. Trim the edges, pressing down well to seal. Decorate the edges of the pie, and cut leaves from the pastry trimmings to decorate the top. Brush with more egg, if using. Bake in the heated oven for 25 to 30 minutes, until golden brown. If the pastry browns too quickly, reduce the oven temperature to moderate (180 C, 350 F, gas 4). *Serves 4*

Note: Since almost all vegetables are suitable for this pie you can use any combination of your favourites, or whatever is most plentiful. Broccoli, French beans, Brussels sprouts, marrow, courgettes and broad beans, whether fresh or frozen, all add colour and flavour. For extra protein, you could stir a few nuts into the vegetable mixture.

The remaining recipes in this chapter are rather special and a little more expensive, but there are many occasions when an extra special meal is called for. Best Roast Lamb is the stuff that best Sunday roast dinners are made of, and now that supermarkets sell frozen game you don't have to live in the country, or be a good shot, to eat Poacher's Pie – rich and full of flavour. Corsican Chicken is reminiscent of holidays in the sun – a beautiful island and plenty of vin de Corse! Why not treat yourself this weekend?

Guinness-braised Steaks with Fondant Potatoes

4 (100 to 175-g/4 to 6-oz) rump steaks
3 large onions, thinly sliced
3 sticks celery, thinly sliced
600 ml/1 pint Guinness
4 tablespoons oil
1 tablespoon flour
150 ml/$\frac{1}{4}$ pint beef stock
bouquet garni
salt and pepper
675 g/1$\frac{1}{2}$ lb large potatoes, peeled

Trim the steaks if necessary to remove any excess fat. Put the steaks into a glass or china bowl with the onion, celery, Guinness and 1 tablespoon of the oil. Cover and leave to marinate in a cool place or in the refrigerator for at least 1 hour, preferably overnight.

Remove the steaks from the marinade and dry them on absorbent kitchen paper. Heat another tablespoon of the oil in a heavy flameproof casserole and brown the steaks on each side over high heat. Remove the steaks from the casserole and reduce the heat. Strain the marinade, reserving the vegetables and liquid. Add the vegetables to the casserole and cook, stirring occasionally, until soft and golden. Stir in the flour and cook until lightly browned. Stir in the liquid from the marinade and the stock. Bring to the boil, stirring constantly. Simmer for 1 minute, then add the steaks and the bouquet garni. Season with a little salt and pepper. Cover and simmer very gently until the steaks are tender – about 1 hour.

Meanwhile, set the oven at hot (220 C, 425 F, gas 7). Slice the potatoes into flat oval discs 1.5 cm/$\frac{3}{4}$ in thick. Heat the remaining oil in a roasting tin. When the oil is very hot add the potatoes – they should lay flat in a single layer. Shake the tin to prevent the potato discs from sticking, then place the tin in the heated oven. Cook, basting frequently, until the undersides of the potato discs are golden brown and crispy – about 20 minutes. Turn the discs over to brown the other side – another 10 minutes.

Pour off the excess fat from the roasting tin and add about 150 ml/$\frac{1}{4}$ pint of the cooking liquid from the steaks; the liquid should come a quarter of the way up the sides of the potatoes. Return the roasting tin to the oven and reduce the heat to moderate (180 C, 350 F, gas 4). Cook, basting frequently, for a further 20 minutes, or until the potatoes are tender when pierced with the tip of a sharp knife. If the tin becomes dry during cooking, add a little more liquid from the steaks.

To serve, arrange the steaks on a deep serving plate and pour over the sauce. Arrange the potatoes in their sauce (which should now be like a sticky glaze) around the edge of the plate.
Serves 4

Poacher's Pie

250 g/9 oz plain flour
3 teaspoons baking powder
$\frac{1}{2}$ teaspoon salt
75 g/3 oz cooked potato, sieved
40 g/1$\frac{1}{2}$ oz butter
1 leek, finely diced
2–3 tablespoons milk

Filling

450 g/1 lb mixed cooked game meat (rabbit, pigeon,
pheasant, grouse, wild duck or venison)
1 tablespoon oil
1 large onion, thinly sliced
100 g/4 oz thick-cut rindless streaky bacon, diced
1 potato, peeled and diced
1 tablespoon redcurrant or rowan jelly
175 ml/6 fl oz strongly flavoured stock
1 tablespoon port
50 g/2 oz mushrooms, quartered
salt and pepper

Set the oven at moderately hot (190 C, 375F, gas 5). Sift the flour, baking powder and salt into a mixing bowl. Rub in the potato and butter until the mixture resembles fine breadcrumbs. Stir in the leek and enough milk to make a soft but not sticky dough. Knead the dough lightly on a floured board and roll it out 8 mm/$\frac{1}{3}$ in thick. Using a 5-cm/2-in plain biscuit cutter, cut out rounds from the dough, re-rolling any trimmings.

Line a greased 900-ml/1$\frac{1}{2}$-pint ovenproof glass pudding basin with the dough rounds, overlapping them slightly so there are no gaps. Reserve eight circles for the top. Cut the game meat into bite-sized pieces. Heat the oil in a saucepan. Add the onion and cook gently until soft. Add the bacon and potato and fry over high heat until the onion, bacon and potato are lightly browned. Stir in the redcurrant or rowan jelly and the stock. Bring to the boil, stirring constantly. Simmer for 2 minutes, then add the port, mushrooms and game meat. Simmer for 5 minutes, then taste for seasoning. Spoon the mixture into the pudding basin and cover with the remaining dough rounds.

Bake the pie in the heated oven for 40 minutes, or until the pastry lining the basin is golden brown on the outside. Turn out the pie and cut it into wedges. If wished, serve with a little extra gravy. *Serves 4–6*

Best Roast Lamb

1 (1.5-kg/3-lb) leg of lamb
3 or 4 cloves garlic, cut into thin slivers
salt and black pepper
few sprigs of fresh rosemary
50 g/2 oz butter, margarine or dripping
1 kg/2 lb large old potatoes, peeled

Set the oven at hot (220 C, 425F, gas 7). Using a small sharp knife, make small slits all over the lamb. Insert a sliver of garlic into each slit. Sprinkle the lamb with salt and pepper and rub into the skin. Place the rosemary sprigs on top of the lamb. Use a little of the fat to grease a large roasting tin or ovenproof baking dish.

Cut the potatoes into 1-cm/½-in slices and lay them in the base of the tin or dish; it doesn't matter if they overlap. Season lightly with salt and pepper (if you really like garlic, you can add a couple of sliced cloves) and dot the top of the potato slices with half the remaining fat. Lay the leg of lamb on the bed of potato slices and dot with the remaining fat.

Roast the lamb and potatoes in the heated oven for 1½ hours, basting frequently. Carve the lamb and serve it, surrounded by the potato slices, with gravy and green vegetables. *Serves 6*

Rich Lamb Ragoût with Dumplings

(Illustrated on page 60)

This dish makes a filling and satisfying meal; serve it with a green salad and a light red wine.

675 g/1½ lb leg of lamb steaks or lean boned lamb, cut
into large cubes
300 ml/½ pint red wine
1 large onion, sliced
2 carrots, sliced
bouquet garni
6 tablespoons oil
1 teaspoon peppercorns
½ tablespoon flour
300 ml/½ pint stock
2 teaspoons tomato purée
salt and pepper
12 baby onions
225 g/8 oz baby carrots, sliced
1 parsnip, diced
2 large potatoes, peeled and diced
Dumplings
100 g/4 oz self-raising flour
1 teaspoon chopped fresh rosemary
1 tablespoon chopped walnuts
50 g/2 oz shredded suet
salt

Put the meat cubes into a glass or china bowl with the wine, sliced onion and carrots, bouquet garni, 2 tablespoons of the oil and the peppercorns. Mix well and leave to marinate for several hours, or overnight.

Set the oven at moderate (180 C, 350 F, gas 4). Strain and reserve the liquid from the marinade. Separate the meat from the vegetables and pat dry. Heat 2 tablespoons of the remaining oil in a heavy flameproof casserole, add the meat and quickly brown it. Remove the meat and add the vegetables from the marinade. Cook until lightly browned, then stir in the flour and cook for 2 minutes, stirring. Stir in the stock, the reserved liquid from the marinade and the tomato purée. Bring to the boil and add salt and pepper to taste. Add the browned meat, stir gently, cover and cook in the heated oven for 1 hour, or until the meat is almost tender. Meanwhile heat the remaining 2 tablespoons of oil in a frying pan and brown the baby onions. Remove and reserve. Put the baby carrots and diced parsnip and potato in a pan, cover with cold water, bring to the boil and simmer for 1 minute, to blanch. Drain and reserve.

To make the dumplings, mix together the flour, rosemary, walnuts, suet, and salt to taste. Mix in enough water – 2 to 3 tablespoons – to form a soft but not sticky dough. Shape the dough into eight dumplings using floured hands.

Remove the meat from the casserole and set aside. Strain the cooking liquid and discard the vegetables (use them in soups or for making gravy). Put the meat and liquid back into the casserole with the baby onions and the blanched vegetables. Cover and cook in the oven for 20 minutes. Taste for seasoning, stir gently and add the dumplings. Cook, uncovered, for a further 10 minutes. *Serves 4*

Lamb and Apricot Casserole

1 (1.5-kg/3-lb) leg of lamb
3 tablespoons oil
25 g/1 oz butter
2 large onions, sliced
1 teaspoon dried sage
$\frac{1}{2}$ teaspoon grated nutmeg
4 tablespoons plain flour
600 ml/1 pint good chicken stock
juice of $\frac{1}{2}$ orange
75 g/3 oz dried apricots, soaked and drained
3 tablespoons raisins
1 teaspoon chopped fresh mint or $\frac{1}{2}$ teaspoon dried
mint (optional)
salt and pepper
450 g/1 lb potatoes

Bone the leg of lamb and cut the meat into 2.5-cm/1-in cubes. Heat the oil and butter in a frying pan and brown the lamb cubes, then place them in a large ovenproof casserole. Add the onions to the frying pan. Stir, then cover and cook gently for about 15 minutes, until soft. Add the sage, nutmeg and flour to the frying pan and cook for another 2 minutes, stirring continuously. Gradually add the stock, orange juice, apricots, raisins, and mint if used. Cook for 2 minutes over a low heat, then pour over the meat. Season to taste. Cut the potatoes into thick slices and arrange on top of the meat mixture.

Cover the casserole and cook for 2 hours in a cool oven (150 C, 300 F, gas 2). Remove the lid and cook for a further 20 minutes, to brown the potatoes. *Serves 4–6*

Clockwise, from the top: Wholewheat Vegetable Pie (page 50); Salmon Salad Loaf (page 45); Sausage Goulash (page 39)

Corsican Chicken

175 g/6 oz rindless back bacon, cut into large dice
1 (1.5-kg/3-lb) chicken
25 g/1 oz butter
225 g/8 oz button mushrooms
3 cloves garlic, or to taste, crushed
1 teaspoon chopped fresh basil or ½ teaspoon dried basil
salt and pepper
1 (400-g/14-oz) can chopped tomatoes
175 ml/6 fl oz chicken stock
50 g/2 oz black olives, stoned
450 g/1 lb small new potatoes, scraped
2 tablespoons brandy

Set the oven at moderately hot (190 C, 375F, gas 5). Put the bacon into a large, heavy casserole and fry it until the fat runs and the bacon is crispy. Remove the bacon and add the chicken and butter to the fat in the casserole. Brown the chicken on all sides. Add the mushrooms, garlic, basil, and salt and pepper to taste, then cover the casserole and cook it in the heated oven for 30 minutes.

Add the tomatoes, stock, olives, potatoes and brandy to the casserole. Stir well, cover and cook for a further 30 minutes. Then remove the lid and cook for another 15 minutes, or until the potatoes are tender. Remove the chicken from the casserole and carve it into six pieces. Taste the sauce and if necessary adjust the seasoning. Spoon the sauce over the chicken and serve immediately. *Serves 6*

From the top: *Chambrette's Potato Gratin (page 110); a mixed salad of cucumber, tomato and Chinese leaf; Rich Lamb Ragoût with Dumplings (page 56)*

61

Savoury Stuffed Roast Chicken

1 (1.5-kg/3-lb) chicken, with giblets
4 large potatoes, peeled
1 chicken stock cube
1 tablespoon chopped fresh thyme or $\frac{1}{2}$ tablespoon
dried thyme
50 g/2 oz butter, softened
salt and pepper
1 large onion, coarsely chopped
300 ml/$\frac{1}{2}$ pint chicken stock or white wine
1–2 teaspoons arrowroot (optional, to thicken)

Set the oven at hot (220 C, 425F, gas 7). Remove the giblets from the chicken and reserve them. Wipe the chicken inside and out. Cut the potatoes into 1-cm/$\frac{1}{2}$-in cubes. Crumble the stock cube and mix it well with the diced potato and half the thyme. Spoon this stuffing into the neck end of the chicken. Spread the butter over the chicken, particularly over the breasts, then sprinkle with a little salt and pepper and with the remaining thyme. Place the chicken in a roasting pan and surround it with the onion and with the neck and crop from the giblets.

Place the chicken in the heated oven and roast it, basting frequently, for 45 minutes. Pour half the stock or wine into the roasting pan and return to the oven for another 15 minutes. Remove the cooked chicken from the pan and carve it into six portions, spooning the stuffing out of the cavity.

To make the gravy, place the roasting pan on top of the stove and bring the pan juices to the boil, stirring well to dislodge any sediment stuck to the sides or base of the pan. Mix the arrowroot, if using, with the remaining stock or wine and add the liquid to the pan. Bring to the boil, stirring constantly. Taste for seasoning and strain into a gravy boat. Serve with the roast chicken and savoury stuffing. *Serves 4–6*

Accompaniments

Most people can't imagine a meal served without potatoes! For them, a meal is just not a meal if there are no spuds; the 'chips with everything' brigade is still alive and well! But potatoes need not mean just chips, mash, boiled or roast. With a little thought and imagination potatoes can be made into any number of interesting vegetable dishes, including several exotic and luxurious ones special enough for when you entertain. Crispy Nut Balls can be prepared in advance and quickly fried before being served with pan-fried trout, chicken Kiev or steaks. Parsnip and Potato Fritters are good with grills or fried egg and bacon and, like Bubble and Squeak, they can be made from left-overs. If you have the time, try making Game Chips – a superior type of crisp and definitely well worth the effort! Stored in a clean, dry biscuit tin in a cool spot they will keep for a couple of weeks, and they are delicious served with drinks, or instead of roast potatoes.

Boiled Potatoes

450 g/1 lb of new potatoes will serve approximately four people; 450 g/1 lb of old potatoes will serve approximately three people.

New Potatoes Scrub new potatoes and place them in a saucepan of cold salted water with a sprig of fresh mint. Bring to the boil, cover the saucepan and cook for 10 to 15 minutes, according to size. They should slide from a sharp knife when cooked. Drain well and serve, dotted with butter and sprinkled with a little chopped mint or parsley.

Old Potatoes Scrub or peel old potatoes and cut them into even-sized pieces. Place them in cold salted water and bring to the boil. Cover the saucepan and simmer the potatoes for 20 to 30 minutes, according to size. Drain well and peel if cooked in their skins. Serve dotted with butter.

Steamed Potatoes Choose small, even-sized potatoes. Peel potatoes thinly and place in a steamer which has a close fitting lid. Bring water to the boil in a saucepan, place the steamer on top and cook for 1 hour, or until tender. Top up the pan with more boiling water from time to time, to prevent it boiling dry. Serve the potatoes dotted with a little butter and seasoning.

Roast Potatoes

675 g–1 kg/1½–2 lb potatoes, peeled
salt
25 g/1 oz plain flour
100 g/4 oz lard or dripping or 150 ml/¼ pint oil

Set the oven at moderately hot (200 C, 400 F, gas 6). Cut the potatoes into large, even-sized chunks. Place them in a saucepan of cold salted water and bring to the boil, then cover the pan and simmer for 2 to 3 minutes. Drain the potatoes thoroughly and put back in the pan. Shake the pan gently over a low heat to make the edges of the potatoes fluffy, then dust them lightly with the flour. Heat the lard or dripping, or the oil, in a roasting tin in the oven. Add the potatoes and baste them with the fat. Roast for 45 minutes to 1 hour, basting occasionally. *Serves 4–6*

Variation
Sugar Roast Potatoes

Omit the flour and dust the potatoes with 50 g/2 oz of soft light-brown sugar. Roast as above until the potatoes are soft and the sugar has caramelized to a deep golden brown.

Sauté Potatoes

450–675 g / 1–1½ lb old potatoes
salt and pepper
75 g /3 oz butter or 50 g /2 oz butter and 2 tablespoons oil
1 tablespoon chopped parsley

Cook the potatoes in their skins, in boiling salted water, for 15 minutes, until just tender. Drain and cool briefly, then peel the potatoes and cut them into 5-mm/¼-in slices. Heat the butter or butter and oil in a heavy-based frying pan and add the potato slices. Fry slowly until golden brown and crisp, shaking the pan frequently and turning the slices occasionally to ensure even browning. Season with salt and pepper and serve, sprinkled with the chopped parsley. *Serves 3–4*

Variation
Lyonnaise Potatoes

Thinly slice 2 onions and fry in a little butter until soft and golden brown. Add to the frying pan just before the potato slices finish cooking.

Chips

675 g/1½ lb old potatoes, peeled
salt
oil for deep frying

Cut the potatoes into 8-mm/⅓-in slices, then cut the slices into 8-mm/⅓-in sticks. (For a more even result first trim each potato into a rectangular block.) Soak the potato sticks in lightly salted water for 30 minutes, then drain them well and dry them thoroughly on absorbent kitchen paper.

Heat oil in a deep fryer to 190 C/375F. Quarter-fill the basket with chips and lower it carefully into the oil. Cook the chips for 7 minutes, until lightly coloured, then remove from the pan and drain on absorbent kitchen paper. Increase the oil temperature to 200 C/400F and fry the chips for another 2 to 3 minutes. Drain again and sprinkle with salt. *Serves 4*

Game Chips

450 g/1 lb potatoes, peeled
oil for deep frying
salt

Trim each potato into an even-sized cylinder; this will give chips which are roughly the same in diameter. Using a sharp knife or mandoline, cut each cylinder into very thin slices. Soak the slices in cold water for 10 minutes to remove excess starch, then drain them and dry thoroughly on absorbent kitchen paper or a clean tea-towel. Deep fry, a few at a time, for 3 minutes at 190 C/375F, or until crisp and golden brown. Remove from the oil, drain on absorbent kitchen paper and sprinkle with salt. *Serves 4*

Puréed Potatoes

1 kg/2 lb potatoes, peeled and cut into large chunks
salt and pepper
150 ml/¼ pint boiling milk
50 g/2 oz butter
grated nutmeg

Cook the potatoes in lightly salted boiling water for 15 minutes, or until tender. Drain thoroughly, then return to the hot pan for a few seconds, to dry off any remaining water. Press the potatoes through a sieve or mash them thoroughly until smooth. Return the mashed potato to the pan and beat in the milk and butter. Add salt, pepper and nutmeg to taste and beat until fluffy. Serve immediately. *Serves 4*

Variations

1. Replace 225 g/8 oz of the potatoes with 225 g/8 oz of peeled and diced celeriac or parsnips. Cook exactly as above.

2. Beat 2 tablespoons chopped parsley (or parsley and chives) into the purée just before serving.

Tip To keep puréed potatoes hot for up to an hour, smooth the surface of the potato purée in the pan and pour on enough cold milk to cover the surface. Cover the pan with a lid and stand the pan in a bain-marie or in a roasting tin half-filled with water and place over a low heat so that the water just simmers. When ready to serve, beat the milk into the purée, turn the purée into a serving dish and smooth the top with a palette knife.

Soufflé Potatoes

450 g / 1 lb uniform-sized potatoes, peeled
oil for deep frying
salt

Cut the potatoes, across or lengthways, into 3-mm/$\frac{1}{8}$-in slices. Leave the slices to soak in cold water for 30 minutes to remove the excess starch. Drain them thoroughly and dry on absorbent kitchen paper. Heat the oil to 120 C/250 F. Quarter-fill a deep frying basket with slices and cook for 3 minutes. Lift them from the pan, drain on absorbent kitchen paper and allow to cool. A few minutes before serving plunge the slices into very hot fat, 220 C/425 F, for 1 minute, or until brown and puffy. *Serves 3–4*

Anna Potatoes

800 g / 1$\frac{3}{4}$ lb even-sized potatoes, peeled
150 g / 2 oz butter, melted
salt and pepper

Set the oven at moderately hot (200 C, 400 F, gas 6). Slice the potatoes thinly. (For a more even result first trim the potatoes into smooth, uniform-sized cylinders.) Grease a flameproof 18 to 20-cm/7 to 8-in baking dish and arrange the first layer of potato slices over the base and sides of the dish in neat concentric circles. Spoon over a little melted butter and season lightly. Continue in this way with the remaining potato slices and melted butter, seasoning each layer. Cover tightly with greased greaseproof paper and foil. Cook over a moderate heat for 10 minutes, then bake in the heated oven for 50 minutes, or until the potatoes are soft when pierced with a skewer. Invert on to a warmed serving plate. *Serves 4–6*

Duchesse Potatoes

450 g / 1 lb potatoes, peeled
salt and pepper
40 g / 1½ oz butter
1 egg, beaten, or 2 egg yolks
1 beaten egg to glaze

Cut the potatoes into even-sized pieces and cook them in boiling salted water for 15 to 20 minutes, until tender. Drain well, return to the pan and dry over a low heat for 1 to 2 minutes. Press the potatoes through a sieve or mash them until smooth, then put them back into the hot pan and beat in the butter, egg or egg yolks and seasoning. Allow the mixture to cool.

Spoon the mixture into a large piping bag fitted with a large star nozzle. Pipe rosettes of the mixture, 5 cm/2 in high, on to a greased baking sheet, bringing the mixture to a point with a quick down and up movement. Brush with beaten egg and bake in a moderately hot oven (200 C, 400 F, gas 6) for 25 minutes or until golden brown. *Serves 4*

Savoury Butters for Baked Potatoes

Instructions for baking potatoes are on page 97.

Snail Butter

French restaurants serve snails in this butter but it is also delicious served with baked potatoes.

100 g/4 oz butter, softened
1 clove garlic, crushed
1 small onion, finely chopped
2 tablespoons dry white wine
2 tablespoons chopped parsley
salt and pepper

Beat together the butter, garlic, onion, wine and parsley, and add salt and pepper to taste.

Marmite Butter

100 g/4 oz unsalted butter, softened
1 teaspoon Marmite or other yeast extract
pepper

Beat together the butter and Marmite and add pepper to taste.

Variation

Replace the Marmite with 1 teaspoonful of Bovril.

Anchovy Butter

1 (50-g/1¾-oz) can anchovy fillets
100 g/4 oz unsalted butter, softened
pepper
1–2 teaspoons lemon juice

Soak the anchovy fillets in cold water for 5 minutes, to remove excess salt. Chop them finely. Beat together the butter and chopped anchovy fillets. Add pepper and lemon juice to taste.

Walnut Butter

100 g/4 oz butter, softened
25 g/1 oz shelled walnuts, chopped
pepper

Beat together the butter and chopped walnuts and add pepper to taste.

Tomato and Sesame Seed Butter

100 g/4 oz butter, softened
1 tablespoon tomato purée
1 tablespoon sesame seeds
salt and pepper

Beat together the softened butter, tomato purée and sesame seeds and add seasoning to taste.

Maître d'Hôtel Butter

100 g/4 oz butter, softened
1 tablespoon finely chopped parsley
2 teaspoons lemon juice
salt and pepper

Beat together the butter, parsley and lemon juice and add seasoning to taste.

Chive Butter

100 g/4 oz butter, softened
1 tablespoon chopped chives
salt and pepper

Beat together the butter and chives and add seasoning to taste.

Caper and Turmeric Butter

100 g/4 oz butter, softened
$\frac{1}{2}$ tablespoon capers, chopped
$\frac{1}{2}$ teaspoon ground turmeric
2 teaspoons mayonnaise
1 tablespoon white wine
pepper

Beat together the butter, capers, turmeric, mayonnaise and wine, and season to taste with pepper.

Crispy Nut Balls

450 g/1 lb mashed potato
50 g/2 oz plain flour
salt and pepper · 1 egg, beaten
50 g/2 oz shelled almonds, finely chopped
oil for deep frying

Divide the mashed potato into 12 portions and, using floured hands, shape each into a small ball. Season the flour with salt and pepper and roll the potato balls in it until lightly coated. Dip each in the beaten egg, then roll in the chopped almonds to give an even coating. Heat the oil to 190 C/375F and deep fry the balls for 2 to 3 minutes, until light golden brown. *Serves 3–4*

Variation

Potato Croquettes

Divide the mashed potato into eight portions and shape each into a cylinder 7.5 cm/3 in long and 1.5 cm/¾ in. in diameter. Replace the almonds with 75 g/3 oz of dry breadcrumbs and deep fry the croquettes for 3 minutes.

Bubble and Squeak

1 small onion, chopped
oil, dripping or bacon fat
450 g/1 lb cooked cabbage, chopped
450 g/1 lb mashed potato
salt and pepper

Fry the onion in a little hot fat until golden. Drain and mix with the cabbage and potato. Season to taste and mould into a round pancake shape. Cook in a little hot fat in a large frying pan until crisp and golden – 4 to 5 minutes each side. Serve with sausages, bacon, chops and fried eggs. *Serves 4–6*

Parmesan Rissoles

450 g/1 lb potatoes, peeled
salt and freshly ground pepper
50 g/2 oz Parmesan cheese, finely grated
15 g/$\frac{1}{2}$ oz butter
25 g/1 oz plain flour
1 egg, beaten
75 g/3 oz day-old breadcrumbs
oil for frying

Cut the potatoes into even-sized pieces and cook in boiling salted water for 15 to 20 minutes. Drain well, then sieve or mash. Beat 40 g/1$\frac{1}{2}$ oz of the cheese, with the butter and seasoning, into the potato purée. With floured hands, divide the mixture into 16 portions and shape each into a small rissole 3.5 cm/1$\frac{1}{2}$ in. in diameter and 1 cm/$\frac{1}{2}$ in high.Dust the rissoles lightly with flour then dip them into the beaten egg. Mix together the breadcrumbs and the remaining cheese and use to coat the rissoles. Heat 5 mm/$\frac{1}{4}$ in of oil in a frying pan until hot and fry the rissoles for 2 minutes on each side, or until golden. *Serves 3–4*

Variation

Replace the Parmesan with 50 g/2 oz of finely diced Cheddar cheese and 50 g/2 oz of roughly chopped Danish salami. Add both to the potato purée and shape the mixture into 20 to 22 small balls. Coat the balls in beaten egg and breadcrumbs and deep fry them for 2 to 3 minutes in oil heated to 190 C/370 F.

Parsnip and Potato Fritters

1 (225-g/8-oz) parsnip, quartered
225 g/8 oz potatoes, peeled, and halved if necessary
salt
15 g/½ oz butter
25 g/1 oz shelled walnuts, coarsely chopped
2 tablespoons flour
1 egg, beaten
oil for frying

Cook the parsnip and potatoes in boiling salted water for about 15 minutes, or untilender. Drain well. Chop the parsnip coarsely and mash the potatoes. Mix together with the butter and walnuts. Shape the mixture into six rounds and coat each in flour then in beaten egg. Shallow fry in hot oil for 3 minutes on each side, until golden brown. Drain on absorbent kitchen paper, sprinkle with salt and serve immediately. *Serves 4–6*

From the top: *Crab Guacamole Salad (page 85); Three Season's Salad (page 86); Potato with Curried Yogurt Dressing (page 89)*

Stelk

This recipe for mashed potatoes with onions comes from Ireland and is wonderful served with sausages or cold meats.

450 g/1 lb onions, sliced
300 ml/½ pint milk
675 g/1½ lb potatoes, peeled
salt and pepper
50 g/2 oz butter
75 g/3 oz grated cheese

Put the onions in a pan and cover them with the milk. Bring to the boil and simmer until tender, about 25 minutes. Meanwhile, cook the potatoes in boiling salted water until tender. Drain the potatoes and mash them thoroughly until smooth. Beat in the onions and milk and add salt and pepper to taste. Then beat in the butter. Turn the mixture into a flameproof serving dish and sprinkle it with the grated cheese. Brown under a hot grill.
Serves 4–6

Baked potato with Niçoise filling. Other fillings, from the top: *Curried chicken; Creamy cheese; Prawn; Smoked haddock; Egg and bacon (pages 97–98)*

Potato Curry

450 g/1 lb potatoes, scrubbed
salt
3 tablespoons oil
1 teaspoon cumin seeds
1 teaspoon mustard seeds
1 teaspoon ground coriander
$\frac{1}{2}$ teaspoon chilli powder
$\frac{1}{2}$ teaspoon ground turmeric
1 (227-g/8-oz) can peeled tomatoes

Boil the potatoes in their skins, in boiling salted water, for 15 minutes. Drain the potatoes, allow to cool, then peel them and cut into small cubes.

Heat the oil in a pan and add the cumin and mustard seeds. As soon as the seeds begin to pop add the coriander, chilli, turmeric, salt to taste, and the tomatoes and their juice. Cook for a few minutes, then stir in 600 ml/1 pint of water. Bring to the boil, reduce the heat and stir in the potatoes. Simmer for 30 minutes and serve immediately. *Serves 3*

Salads

Think of salads and you usually think of lettuce, cucumber and tomato – the basis of summertime meals. But salads don't have to be predictable: potato salads can make a wonderful change! They don't have to be fattening either; it all depends on what you put on your salad. After all, even lettuce is fattening when drenched in olive oil or mayonnaise. Potato salads can also be more filling than traditional green salads, so you won't feel hungry so soon. This chapter contains a selection of potato salads for all occasions and seasons. Try Potato with Curried Yogurt Dressing for a spicy change, or Sesame Crunch Salad, which looks what it is – healthy! For something a bit more filling there is Smoked Mackerel Salad and Hot Chicken Liver and Potato Salad, each a meal in itself. If you like hot spicy food from China, try Szechwan-style Potato Salad, served with cold meats. Crab Guacamole Salad is another exotic one, and is perfect for summer entertaining, barbecues and meals on a patio.

Potato and Pepperoni Salad

450 g/1 lb small new potatoes
salt and pepper
225 g/8 oz pepperoni sausage, sliced
1 tablespoon chopped basil or chives
4 tomatoes, peeled and quartered
1 black sweet pepper, cored and sliced
150 ml/$\frac{1}{4}$ pint olive oil or vegetable oil, or a mixture of
both
1–2 tablespoons white wine vinegar
1 clove garlic, crushed
$\frac{1}{4}$ teaspoon mustard powder
1 cos lettuce

Cook the potatoes in boiling salted water for 15 minutes, or until just tender. Drain, cool briefly, then peel. Put the warm or cold potatoes into a large bowl. Set the oven at moderate (180 C, 350 F, gas 4). Arrange the slices of pepperoni on a baking sheet or in a roasting tin and put in the oven for 5 minutes, to heat through. Add to the potatoes with the basil or chives, tomato quarters and sliced pepper. Mix together the oil, vinegar, garlic and mustard, and add salt and pepper to taste. Pour the vinaigrette over the potato salad and toss well to mix. Tear the lettuce leaves into thirds and arrange them in the base of a large salad bowl or on a serving plate. Arrange the potato mixture on top and serve with crusty bread. *Serves 4–6*

Hot Chicken Liver and Potato Salad

3 large potatoes, scrubbed
salt and pepper
4 rindless rashers streaky bacon
225 g/8 oz chicken livers
3 tablespoons oil
3 tablespoons wine vinegar
1 iceberg lettuce, torn into 5-cm/2-in pieces

Cook the potatoes in their skins, in boiling salted water, for about 20 minutes, or until tender. Drain and leave until cool enough to handle. Peel the potatoes and cut them into thick slices. Put the slices into a large ovenproof serving bowl.

Cut the bacon into 2.5-cm/1-in square pieces and fry in a heavy frying pan until crisp and brown. Add the bacon to the potatoes, leaving any fat behind in the pan. Trim the chicken livers if necessary, and cut them in half. Add the oil to the bacon fat left in the frying pan and heat. When the fat is hot, add the chicken livers and fry, stirring constantly, for 2 minutes, until brown but not hard. Tip the livers and the oil on to the potato and bacon mixture and toss to mix. Add the vinegar to the hot pan and bring to the boil, stirring constantly to dislodge any meat juices stuck to the pan; as you do this stand away from the fumes, which are very strong. Pour the boiling vinegar over the potato mixture and toss gently. Season lightly with a very little salt, and some pepper to taste. Add the lettuce, toss again and serve immediately. *Serves 4*

Smoked Mackerel Salad

675 g/1½ lb small new potatoes, scrubbed
salt and black pepper
4 fillets smoked mackerel
juice of 1 lemon
1 tablespoon vegetable oil
1 tablespoon chopped parsley

Cook the potatoes in boiling salted water for 15 minutes, or until tender, then drain and allow to cool. Peel the potatoes and arrange them in a salad bowl. Flake the fish and pile on top of the potatoes. Mix the lemon juice and oil together and season with plenty of black pepper – there will be enough salt in the fish to flavour the salad. Pour the dressing over and sprinkle with the parsley. *Serves 4*

Sesame Crunch Salad

4 large potatoes, peeled
salt and pepper
4 large carrots
1 (150-g/5.3-oz) carton natural yogurt
1 or 2 cloves garlic, crushed
25 g/1 oz sesame seeds
25 g/1 oz raisins

Cut the potatoes into 5-mm/¼-in dice and cook in boiling salted water for 5 minutes, or until just tender. Drain and cool. Grate the carrots coarsely. Tip the yogurt into a large mixing bowl, add the garlic and salt and pepper, and whisk until smooth. Stir in the potatoes, carrots, sesame seeds and raisins. Cover tightly and chill. To serve, spoon into a salad bowl and serve with crusty bread. *Serves 4*

Crab Guacamole Salad

(Illustrated on page 77)

450 g / 1 lb new potatoes, scrubbed
salt and pepper
2 ripe avocados
1 small onion, grated or very finely chopped
1 small green pepper, deseeded and finely diced
1 tablespoon lemon juice
1 (198-g / 7-oz) can crabmeat
Tabasco sauce

Cook the potatoes in boiling salted water for 15 minutes, or until tender. Drain the potatoes, dice and cool them.

Peel and mash the avocados and stir in the onion, green pepper, lemon juice, crabmeat and the cooled potatoes. Season to taste with salt, pepper and a few drops of Tabasco. Chill until needed, then serve with a green salad and crusty bread. *Serves 4, or 6 as a starter.*

New York Salad

675 g / 1½ lb small new or old potatoes, scrubbed
salt and pepper
4 spring onions, sliced
300 ml / ½ pint soured cream
chopped chives to garnish (optional)

Cook the potatoes in boiling salted water for 15 to 20 minutes, or until tender. Drain and leave to cool, then peel. Small potatoes should be left whole; larger ones should be cut into chunks. Mix the spring onions and soured cream in a large bowl. Carefully stir in the potatoes and season to taste. Spoon into a salad bowl and serve, sprinkled with chives. *Serves 4–6*

Three Season's Salad

(Illustrated on page 77)

3 potatoes, scrubbed
salt and pepper
3 sticks celery
1 large beetroot, cooked and peeled
150 ml/¼ pint mayonnaise
lemon juice
lettuce leaves (optional)
1 tablespoon chopped chives

Cook the potatoes in their skins, in boiling salted water, for about 20 minutes, or until just tender. Drain and allow to cool. Peel the potatoes and cut them into 1-cm/½-in dice. Cut the celery and beetroot into similar-sized dice. Mix the potato, celery and beetroot cubes and fold in the mayonnaise. Season to taste with salt, pepper and a little lemon juice. Spoon the mixture into a serving bowl lined with lettuce leaves, if liked, and sprinkle with the chives. Serve with cold meat and poultry.
Serves 4

Variation

Add 1 tart eating apple, cored and diced, to the salad.

Szechwan-style Potato Salad

450 g/1 lb small new potatoes, scrubbed
salt
2 or 3 cloves garlic, crushed
2 dried chilli peppers, crushed
6 tablespoons sesame oil or vegetable oil
6 tablespoons white wine vinegar
25 g/1 oz caster sugar

Cook the potatoes in boiling salted water for 15 minutes, or until tender. Drain and transfer to an ovenproof serving bowl, with the garlic and peppers. Heat the oil until it begins to smoke and pour it over the potato mixture. Bring the vinegar to the boil and pour it over the potatoes. Sprinkle on the sugar and a little salt and toss the salad well. Cover and leave to marinate for as long as possible, preferably overnight. *Serves 4–6*

Potato Vinaigrette

675 g/1½ lb small new potatoes, scrubbed
salt and pepper
1 onion, finely chopped
2 tablespoons chopped parsley
1 tablespoon chopped chives or mint, or another herb
of your choice
150 ml/¼ pint vegetable oil or olive oil
2 tablespoons wine vinegar
¼ teaspoon mustard powder

Cook the potatoes in boiling salted water for 15 minutes, or until just tender. Drain and leave until cool enough to handle. Meanwhile, mix together the chopped onion, parsley and other herbs. Whisk together the oil, vinegar and mustard, and add salt and pepper to taste. Add the dressing to the onion herb mixture.

Peel the warm potatoes and cut them in half. Mix in the onion dressing and taste for seasoning. The salad will taste better if the potatoes are still warm. Spoon the salad into a serving bowl and allow to stand for 2 hours before serving. *Serves 4*

Potato with
Curried Yogurt Dressing

(Illustrated on page 77)

6 large potatoes, peeled and cut into 1-cm/$\frac{1}{2}$-in dice
salt and pepper
1 teaspoon curry powder, or to taste
2 teaspoons mango or other chutney
1 (150-g/5.3-oz) carton natural yogurt
1 hard-boiled egg

Garnish

few slices of cucumber
small bunch of watercress or a few chopped chives

Cook the potatoes in boiling salted water for 5 minutes, or until just tender. Drain and cool. Stir the curry powder and chutney into the yogurt and add salt and pepper to taste. Stir in the diced potatoes. Halve the egg and separate the white from the yolk. Push the white and yolk, separately, through a sieve. Arrange the potato mixture in a bowl and sprinkle or spoon the sieved egg white and yolk on top to make an attractive pattern. Cut the cucumber slices in half and arrange them round the edge of the bowl. Decorate with a few sprigs of watercress or a few chopped chives. *Serves 4*

Dordogne Salad

4 large potatoes, scrubbed
salt and pepper
4 sticks celery
3 tablespoons oil
1 tablespoon wine vinegar
$\frac{1}{8}$ teaspoon mustard powder
25 g/1 oz walnuts, coarsely chopped
100 g/4 oz Roquefort cheese, crumbled

Cook the potatoes in boiling salted water for 20 to 30 minutes, or until tender. Drain, peel, halve and thickly slice the potatoes while still warm. Place the slices in a salad bowl. Cut the celery into matchsticks and add to the potato. Whisk together the oil, vinegar and mustard powder and add salt and pepper to taste. Pour over the potato and celery. Mix gently and top with the chopped walnuts and crumbled cheese. *Serves 4*

Supper Dishes

Potatoes form the ideal basis for supper dishes: as well as being cheap and nutritious, they can quickly be transformed into a tasty, filling, hot meal. Magic! And just what is needed after a hectic day.

If you are lucky enough to have a microwave oven, it takes only five minutes to bake a potato in its skin. Add your favourite filling and there is your meal, in a baked potato! Dishes such as Potato Quiche Lorraine, Pepperoni Pizza and Kipper Flan can all be made in advance, chilled or frozen, and then quickly reheated when needed.

Finally, for the ultimate in potato cookery, try Chambrette's Potato Gratin – a gourmet's treat!

Savoury Croquettes

Lamb and Apricot

450 g/1 lb mashed potato
175 g/6 oz cooked lamb, minced
75 g/3 oz dried apricots, finely chopped
salt and pepper
3 tablespoons plain flour
1 egg, beaten
150 g/5 oz fresh breadcrumbs
oil for frying

Mix the potato with the minced lamb and chopped apricots and season to taste with salt and pepper. Shape the mixture into 16 croquettes. Roll them in flour, dip them in the beaten egg and finally coat them thoroughly in breadcrumbs. Chill until ready to use. Heat about 1 cm/½ in of oil in a frying pan and fry the croquettes for about 5 minutes, turning constantly so they cook evenly. When the croquettes are golden brown and crisp, remove from the pan and drain on absorbent kitchen paper.
Serves 4

Beef and Pepper

Follow the recipe for Lamb and Apricot croquettes, replacing the lamb with 175 g/6 oz minced cooked beef (or use minced beef that has been lightly fried, drained and cooled). Replace the apricots with half a red pepper, deseeded and diced.

Pork and Apple

Follow the recipe for Lamb and Apricot croquettes, replacing the lamb with 175 g/6 oz of minced cooked pork. Replace the apricots with a quarter of a cooking apple, peeled, cored and chopped, and 1 small onion, finely chopped.

Chicken and Walnut

Follow the recipe for Lamb and Apricot croquettes, replacing the lamb with 175 g/6 oz of minced cooked chicken. Replace the apricots with 50 g/2 oz of chopped walnuts.

Cheese

Follow the recipe for Lamb and Apricot croquettes, replacing the lamb with 175 g/6 oz of diced cheese; Gruyère is excellent but Cheddar, Camembert and Stilton are also very good. Omit the apricots and beat in 1 egg yolk, and season with very little salt but plenty of black pepper. If you wish, replace 1 tablespoon of the breadcrumbs (for the coating) with 1 tablespoon of grated Parmesan cheese.

Cheese and Ham

Follow the recipe for Cheese croquettes, adding 50 g/2 oz of diced ham to the cheese and potato mixture.

Bacon Potato Cakes

2 eggs, beaten
1 tablespoon chopped parsley
salt and pepper
1 kg/2 lb hot mashed potato
175 g/6 oz rindless streaky bacon, chopped, or cold
boiled bacon, finely diced
50 g/2 oz plain flour
50 g/2 oz muesli
50 g/2 oz Scottish oat flakes with bran
8 fried eggs

Beat 1 of the eggs, the parsley and seasoning into the mashed potato. Fry the streaky bacon (if using) until crispy and stir it or the boiled bacon into the potato. Using floured hands, divide the mixture into 8 flat cakes and dust them lightly with the flour.

Mix the muesli and oat flakes. Coat the potato cakes with the remaining beaten egg and then with the muesli and oat flake mixture. Cook on a lightly greased griddle or in a greased heavy-based frying pan for about 3 minutes on each side. Top each potato cake with 1 fried egg and serve immediately. *Serves 4*

From the top: *Florentine Pancakes (page 108); Pepperoni Pizza (page 101); Kipper Flan (page 106)*

Stuffed Baked Potatoes

(Illustrated on page 78)

4 (225-g/8-oz) unblemished potatoes
1–2 tablespoons oil · salt

Set the oven at moderately hot (200 C, 400 F, gas 6). Scrub the potatoes very thoroughly and pat them dry with absorbent kitchen paper. Brush with a little oil and sprinkle with salt, then place in a roasting tin making sure that they don't touch. Bake in the oven for 1 hour, or until soft when squeezed. Split the potatoes in half and serve with one of the fillings below. Each filling is sufficient for four potatoes. *Serves 4*

Smoked haddock Cook, skin and flake 225 g/8 oz of smoked haddock fillets. Mix with 1 hard-boiled egg, mashed, and 4 tablespoons of single or double cream. Season with plenty of black pepper.

Creamy cheese Mix 100 g/4 oz of cream cheese with 2 tablespoons of sweet pickle. Sprinkle on a little paprika.

Egg and bacon Crumble 8 rashers of grilled bacon. Combine with 2 eggs, boiled for 7 minutes and shelled and mashed while still warm.

Niçoise Cook 100 g/4 oz of French beans, drain and cut into 2.5-cm/1-in pieces. Mix these with 2 sliced tomatoes, 2 sliced hard-boiled eggs, 2 chopped anchovy fillets and halved and stoned black olives. Moisten with a little olive oil and season to taste with black pepper.

Soured cream and chives Mix 150 ml/$\frac{1}{4}$ pint of soured cream with 2 tablespoons chopped chives. Season with sea salt and freshly ground pepper.

Clockwise, from the top: Apple Scone (page 120); Rum Truffles (page 116); Fudge Ring (page 121); Coconut Ice (page 115)

Soured cream and caviar   The ultimate filling for baked potatoes! Stir pressed caviar, lumpfish roe or smoked cod's roe into 150 ml/¼ pint of soured cream.

Prawn   Mix 150 ml/¼ pint of mayonnaise with 2 tablespoons of tomato ketchup and a couple of drops of Tabasco sauce. Stir in 175 g/6 oz of peeled cooked prawns and 1 tablespoon of chopped parsley.

Curried chicken   Chop 225 g/8 oz of cold cooked chicken. Finely chop 1 small onion and fry it until soft in 25 g/1 oz of butter. Add 3 teaspoons of curry powder, or to taste, and fry, stirring, for 1 minute. Add 5 tablespoons of tomato juice and 1 tablespoon of mango chutney. Simmer for 2 minutes. Cool and stir into 150 ml/¼ pint of mayonnaise, with the chopped chicken.

Poached egg hollandaise   Mash 100 g/4 oz of butter until soft. Whisk 2 egg yolks with 15 g/½ oz of the butter in a small pan. Over a very low heat or in a bain-marie, whisk in 1 teaspoon of lemon juice and a large pinch of salt. Continue whisking until the mixture has thickened slightly then gradually whisk in the remaining butter, a little at a time, whisking until the sauce is very thick. Taste for seasoning and keep warm. Poach 4 eggs. Place 1 egg inside each potato and top with the hollandaise sauce.

Soufflé   Scoop out the hot potato taking care not to tear the skin. Mash the potato with 50 g/2 oz of butter, 3 tablespoons of double cream, 2 egg yolks, 50 g/2 oz of grated cheese and salt and pepper to taste. Fold in 2 stiffly beaten egg whites. Carefully spoon into the potato skins and sprinkle with 25 g/1 oz of grated cheese. Place in an ovenproof dish and bake in a moderately hot oven (190 C, 375 F, gas 5) for 15 minutes.

Iced Camembert   Carefully remove the skin from 4 Camembert portions and mash the cheese with 2 tablespoons of dry white wine. Leave for 2 hours, pour off the excess wine, then beat in 25 g/1 oz of unsalted butter and pepper to taste. Pack the cheese into a small, freezer-proof dish and place in the freezer for 1 hour before serving.

Potato Feuilleté

This traditional French pie is sold in charcuteries in Burgundy. There are many different variations: some have ham or cooked bacon added, some omit the herbs and add garlic. This version, my favourite, has cheese, herbs and soured cream.

1 (368-g/13-oz) packet frozen puff pastry, thawed
450 g/1 lb large potatoes, peeled and thinly sliced
1 tablespoon chopped chives
1 tablespoon chopped parsley
100 g/4 oz Roquefort cheese, crumbled
1 egg, beaten
150 ml/¼ pint soured cream
pepper

Set the oven at hot (220 C, 425F, gas 7). Roll out the pastry as thinly as possible and cut it in half. Use one half of the pastry to line a deep 23-cm/9-in pie plate. Cover the base with a thin layer of potato slices and sprinkle with a few chopped herbs. Then cover with another thin layer of potato slices and sprinkle with a little cheese. Continue layering until all the potato slices, herbs and cheese are used up, finishing with a layer of potatoes. Dampen the pastry rim and cover the pie with the remaining pastry. Trim the edges and press them together to seal. Decorate with leaves cut from the trimmings. Cut a hole in the centre of the pie.

Brush the pie with beaten egg and bake it in the heated oven for 15 minutes, until risen and golden. Reduce the oven temperature to moderate (180 C, 350F, gas 4) and cook for a further 30 minutes. If the pie browns too quickly during baking, cover it with foil or greaseproof paper.

Mix the soured cream with a little pepper – no salt is needed as the cheese is already salty. Pour the seasoned cream into the pie through the hole in the top; use a small metal funnel, piping tube or nozzle. Serve the pie immediately, with a tossed green salad. *Serves 6*

Spiced Meat Puffs

675 g / 1½ lb potatoes, peeled
salt and pepper
25 g / 1 oz butter
150 g / 5 oz fresh breadcrumbs (wholemeal taste best)
75 g / 3 oz plain flour
2 eggs
225 g / 8 oz cold cooked meat, minced (chicken, pork,
lamb or beef)
2 tablespoons tomato ketchup
1 small red pepper, deseeded and finely chopped
1 red or green chilli pepper, deseeded and finely
chopped
oil for deep frying

Cook the potatoes in boiling salted water for 20 minutes, or until tender. Drain very thoroughly then mash until smooth. Stir in the butter, 50 g / 2 oz of the breadcrumbs, the flour, salt and pepper and 1 beaten egg. Work the mixture into a dough that is firm and not sticky, using a little extra flour if necessary. Chill the dough for 30 minutes, then roll it out on a floured work surface, 5 mm / ¼ in thick, into a 30-cm / 12-in square. Cut the large square into nine 10-cm / 4-in smaller squares.

Mix the meat with the ketchup, peppers and a little salt. Divide the mixture between the squares. Brush the edges of each square with beaten egg and fold over to make a triangle. Press the edges firmly to seal. Coat the triangles with the remaining beaten egg and then dip them in the remaining breadcrumbs.

Heat oil to 185 C / 365 F and deep fry the puffs, a few at a time, until golden brown – about 4 minutes. *Serves 4–6*

Variation

Fill each square with a teaspoonful of apricot jam and fry as above. Sprinkle the cooked puffs with cinnamon-flavoured caster sugar and serve with custard or ice cream.

Pepperoni Pizza

(Illustrated on page 95)

Topping
1 tablespoon vegetable or olive oil
1 onion, chopped
1 (397-g/14-oz) can chopped tomatoes
1 clove garlic, crushed
2 teaspoons dried oregano
salt and pepper
100 g/4 oz mozzarella or Cheddar cheese, thinly sliced
(optional)
1 (100-g/4-oz) piece pepperoni sausage
Base
225 g/8 oz potatoes, peeled
salt
175 g/6 oz plain flour
4 teaspoons baking powder
40 g/1½ oz butter, cut into cubes

First make the topping. Heat the oil and fry the onion gently until soft but not browned. Add the tomatoes, garlic and oregano and season lightly with salt and pepper. Cook, uncovered, until very thick – about 20 minutes. Meanwhile prepare the base.

Cook the potatoes in boiling salted water for 20 to 30 minutes, until tender. Drain thoroughly, then rub through a sieve and leave to cool. Sift the flour, ½ teaspoon of salt and the baking powder into a bowl. Add the butter and rub into the flour until the mixture resembles fine breadcrumbs. Add the potatoes and knead to form a soft dough. On a floured board, roll out the dough 8 mm/⅓ in thick and shape it into a 20-cm/8-in circle.

Set the oven at moderate (180 C, 350 F, gas 4). Place the dough base on a greased baking sheet and spread it evenly with the tomato mixture. Arrange the slices of cheese on top, if using, and then the pepperoni. Bake in the heated oven for 25 minutes. Cut into wedges and serve immediately. *Serves 6*

Quick Beef Hash

675 g/1½ lb potatoes, peeled
salt and pepper
2 tablespoons oil
2 onions, sliced into rings
4 tablespoons hot milk
1 (340-g/12-oz) can corned beef, coarsely chopped
1 (225-g/7.94-oz) can curried baked beans

Cook the potatoes in boiling salted water for 20 to 30 minutes, or until tender. Drain thoroughly, then mash until smooth. Meanwhile, heat the oil in a frying pan, add the onions and fry until golden brown.

Beat the hot milk into the mashed potato, then stir in the corned beef, onions and beans. Season to taste, then return the mixture to the frying pan. Fry over a high heat, turning constantly, until crispy and golden. *Serves 4*

Chorizo Fry-up

3 tablespoons vegetable oil
1 onion, chopped
4 large cooked potatoes, thickly sliced
225 g/8 oz chorizo sausage, thinly sliced
1 (283-g/10-oz) can sweet corn
1 tablespoon chopped parsley

Heat the oil in a large frying pan. Add the onion and cook gently until soft but not coloured. Increase the heat and add the potatoes and fry, stirring frequently, until crisp and golden. Stir in the chorizo and sweet corn and fry for 2 minutes more. Sprinkle with the parsley and serve at once. *Serves 4*

Creamy Fish Fondue

4 large potatoes, peeled and halved
salt and black pepper
225 g/8 oz smoked haddock fillets, cooked, skinned and
flaked
150 ml/¼ pint soured cream
3 tablespoons milk
50 g/2 oz butter
100 g/4 oz Gruyère or strong Cheddar cheese, grated

Cook the potatoes in boiling salted water for 20 to 25 minutes, until tender. Drain thoroughly then push through a sieve or mash very thoroughly. Over a low heat, beat the fish into the mashed potato with the cream, milk and butter. Then beat in the cheese and season to taste with black pepper. Transfer the mixure to a fondue pan or flameproof pot placed over a table burner. Serve with cubes of crusty granary bread, raw cauliflower florets, and sliced carrots, courgettes, celery and cucumber. Each person spears a cube of bread or one of the vegetables on to his fondue fork, then dips it into the fondue pan until thoroughly coated. *Serves 4*

103

Smoked Haddock Fish Cakes with Spicy Sauce

450 g/1 lb mashed potato
225 g/8 oz smoked Haddock fillets, cooked, skinned and
flaked
salt and pepper
3 tablespoons plain flour
1 egg, beaten
75 g/3 oz fresh breadcrumbs
oil for frying
Spicy Sauce
15 g/$\frac{1}{2}$ oz butter
1 onion, finely chopped
1 teaspoon plain flour
1 (400-g/14-oz) can chopped tomatoes
1 tablespoon chopped parsley
few drops of Tabasco sauce
few drops of Worcestershire sauce
salt and pepper

To make the fish cakes, beat the potato until smooth and free of lumps. Beat the fish into the potato and season to taste. Using floured hands, shape the mixture into eight small cakes. Coat the fish cakes in flour, dip them in beaten egg and finally roll them in the breadcrumbs, making sure they are completely coated. Chill in the refrigerator until firm.

Heat 1 cm/$\frac{1}{2}$ in of oil in a frying pan and fry the fish cakes for 3 to 4 minutes on each side, until golden brown and crisp. Drain on absorbent kitchen paper and serve with Spicy Sauce.

To make the Spicy Sauce, melt the butter in a pan, add the onion and cook gently, stirring occasionally, until soft but not browned – about 15 minutes. Stir in the flour, then the tomatoes, and bring to the boil. Simmer gently for about 10 minutes, until fairly thick. Stir in the chopped parsley and Tabasco sauce and Worcestershire sauce to taste. Taste for seasoning and add salt and pepper if necessary. Spicy Sauce may also be served with Savoury Croquettes (page 92). *Serves 4*

Variations
Sardine Fish Cakes

Follow the main recipe, replacing the smoked haddock with 1 (120-g/4¼-oz) can of sardines in tomato sauce, mashed.

Tuna Fish Cakes

Follow the main recipe, replacing the smoked haddock with 1 (198-g/7-oz) can of tuna in oil. Mash the tuna with a little of the oil from the can and proceed as above.

Crunchy Salmon Pie

450 g/1 lb potatoes, peeled
salt and pepper
4 tablespoons hot milk
25 g/1 oz butter
1 (439-g/15½-oz) can salmon, flaked
2 tomatoes, peeled, deseeded and diced
1 tablespoon chopped chives or parsley
2 hard-boiled eggs, chopped
1 (425-g/15-oz) can smoked salmon soup
1 packet salted plain crisps, lightly crushed

Set the oven at moderately hot (190 C, 375F, gas 5). Cook the potatoes in boiling salted water for 20 minutes, or until tender. Drain and mash thoroughly until smooth. Beat in the hot milk and the butter, then season the purée lightly with salt and pepper. Mix the salmon with the tomatoes, herbs, eggs and soup. Spoon the mixture into a shallow ovenproof baking dish and spread the potato purée on top. Sprinkle on the crisps. Bake in the heated oven for 15 to 20 minutes, until golden brown. *Serves 4*

Kipper Flan

(Illustrated on page 95)

Pastry

175 g/6 oz wholemeal flour

pinch of salt

25 g/1 oz lard

50 g/2 oz butter

Filling

225 g/8 oz kipper fillets, cooked

175 g/6 oz mashed potato

25 g/1 oz butter

1 egg, beaten

4 tablespoons single cream

black pepper

75 g/3 oz cheese (Cheddar, Brie or any leftovers),

grated or finely sliced

1 (50-g/1¾-oz) can anchovy fillets, drained

To make the pastry, sift the flour and salt into a mixing bowl and rub in the lard and butter with your fingertips until the mixture resembles fine breadcrumbs. Stir in enough water – 2 to 3 tablespoons – to make a soft but not sticky dough. Wrap the dough in greaseproof paper and chill it in the refrigerator for 20 minutes while you make the filling. Set the oven at moderately hot (190 C, 375F, gas 5).

To make the filling, mash together the kipper fillets and potato until smooth. Beat in the butter, egg and cream and season to taste with black pepper.

Roll out the chilled dough on a lightly floured surface and use it to line a 23-cm/9-in flan case. Spoon in the filling and top with the cheese. Bake in the heated oven for 20 to 25 minutes, or until lightly browned and set. Before serving, cut the anchovy fillets in half lengthways, then cut each into two or three pieces. Arrange the pieces round the edge of the flan in a decorative pattern. Serve warm, with a mixed salad. *Serves 4–6*

Gnocchi

1 kg/2 lb large potatoes, scrubbed
100 g/4 oz butter
2 eggs
1 egg yolk
150 g/5 oz plain flour
2 tablespoons grated Parmesan cheese
salt and pepper
Sauce
25 g/1 oz butter
25 g/1 oz plain flour
300 ml/$\frac{1}{2}$ pint creamy milk
salt and pepper
100 g/4 oz grated Cheddar cheese

Set the oven at moderately hot (190 C, 375F, gas 5). Prick the potatoes with a fork and bake them in the heated oven for 1 to 1$\frac{1}{2}$ hours, until tender. Cool the potatoes slightly, then peel them and rub the insides through a sieve or mash thoroughly. Beat in the butter, whole eggs, egg yolk, flour and cheese. Season to taste and allow to cool.

To make the sauce, melt the butter in a pan and stir in the flour. Remove the pan from the heat and gradually stir in the milk. Return to the heat and bring to the boil, stirring constantly. Simmer gently for 2 minutes. Season to taste and stir in half the grated cheese. Keep warm while you poach the gnocchi.

Bring a pan of lightly salted water to the boil and poach heaped teaspoonfuls of the mixture for 5 minutes; this will have to be done in several batches. Drain the gnocchi on absorbent kitchen paper and arrange them in a greased ovenproof baking dish. Spoon over the cheese sauce and sprinkle with the remaining grated cheese. Place under a heated grill for 2 minutes, until golden brown and bubbling. *Serves 4*

Florentine Pancakes

(Illustrated on page 95)

Pancakes
225 g/8 oz cooked potato, sieved
150 g/5 oz plain flour
salt
4 eggs, separated
600 ml/1 pint milk
oil
Filling
100 g/4 oz butter
2 (227-g/8-oz) packets frozen chopped spinach
225 g/8 oz ricotta cheese
100 g/4 oz diced ham or cooked bacon (optional)
salt and pepper
grated nutmeg

First make the pancakes. Mix together the potato, flour and a little salt. Make a well in the centre of this mixture, add the egg yolks beaten with the milk, and gradually stir to make a smooth batter. Stiffly beat the egg whites and fold into the mixture. Lightly oil a small (preferably non-stick) frying pan or pancake pan. Add enough batter to the heated pan just to cover the base, and cook until golden brown. Loosen the pancake with a palette knife and toss or turn it to cook the other side. Slide the cooked pancake on to a plate, then cook the remaining batter in the same way. The batter should make about 10 pancakes.

To make the filling, melt 50 g/2 oz of the butter, add the frozen spinach and cook slowly, stirring frequently, until thawed. Bring to the boil and cook slowly until all the excess water has evaporated. Remove the pan from the heat and stir in the ricotta, and the ham or bacon if using. Season to taste with salt, pepper and grated nutmeg. Place 1 heaped tablespoon of filling in the centre of each pancake and roll up. Arrange the pancakes in a greased ovenproof baking dish and dot with the remaining butter. Heat briefly in the oven until lightly browned, 5 to 7 minutes. Serve with a cheese sauce, if liked. *Serves 4*

Variation

Replace the spinach and cheese filling with one made from eggs and prawns. Coarsely chop 5 hard-boiled eggs and mix with 100 g/4 oz of peeled cooked prawns. Make a white sauce using 25 g/1 oz of butter, 25 g/1 oz of plain flour and 450 ml/¾ pint of milk. Stir in the eggs and prawns and season. Use to stuff the pancakes and continue as above.

Hearty Spanish Omelette

4 eggs, beaten
1 small onion, chopped
50 g/2 oz cooked peas
4 tablespoons single or double cream
1 small red pepper, deseeded and diced
1 tomato, peeled and diced
50 g/2 oz cooked green beans
100 g/4 oz sliced chorizo sausage or ham, cooked and diced bacon, diced cooked chicken, prawns, or a mixture of some of these
2 large cooked potatoes, diced
1 or 2 cloves garlic, crushed (optional)
salt and pepper
2 tablespoons olive oil or vegetable oil

Mix the beaten eggs with all the other ingredients except the oil. Heat the oil in a large 25 to 30-cm/10 to 12-in non-stick frying pan. Pour in the egg mixture and stir with a fork so the outer edges which set first are drawn to the centre and the uncooked mixture flows to the edges of the pan. Stop stirring when the mixture is almost set and allow the base of the omelette to brown slightly. Place a large plate over the pan and invert it so the omelette falls on to the plate. Slip the omelette back into the pan, browned side uppermost, and brown the other side. Cut into wedges and serve immediately. This omelette is also tasty served cold, with salad. *Serves 2–4*

Chambrette's Potato Gratin

(Illustrated on page 60)

600 ml/1 pint milk
1 kg/2 lb potatoes, peeled and thinly sliced
salt and pepper
1 clove garlic
150 ml/$\frac{1}{4}$ pint soured cream
150 ml/$\frac{1}{4}$ pint double cream
grated nutmeg
175 g/6 oz Gruyère or strong Cheddar cheese, grated

Bring the milk and 150 ml/$\frac{1}{4}$ pint of water to the boil in a large pan. Add the potato slices and season lightly. Simmer very gently for about 10 minutes, until half cooked but still firm. Drain the potatoes, reserving the milk for soup. Cut the clove of garlic into pieces and rub over the base and sides of an ovenproof baking dish. Grease the dish with butter and set the oven at moderately hot (200 C, 400F, gas 6).

Bring the soured cream and double cream to the boil in a pan. Add the potato slices, and salt, pepper and grated nutmeg to taste. Simmer gently for 10 minutes, shaking the pan occasionally to prevent the potatoes from sticking. Place one-third of the potatoes and cream in the baking dish and sprinkle with one-third of the cheese. Continue layering until all the potatoes and cream and cheese have been used, finishing with a layer of cheese. Bake in the heated oven for 20 minutes, until bubbling and golden brown. *Serves 4*

Variation

Drain 1 (50-g/1$\frac{3}{4}$-oz) can of anchovies and soak the anchovies in a little milk to remove the excess salt. Replace the first two layers of cheese with strips of anchovy fillets. Sprinkle the top layer of potatoes with 50 g/2 oz of grated cheese and bake as above.

Potato Quiche Lorraine

Pastry
175 g/6 oz plain flour
pinch of salt
25 g/1 oz lard, cut into cubes
50 g/2 oz butter, cut into cubes
Filling
100 g/4 oz cold mashed potato
2 eggs, beaten
300 ml/½ pint milk
100 g/4 oz Cheddar cheese, grated
15 g/½ oz butter
1 small onion, finely chopped
75 g/3 oz ham or bacon, diced

First make the pastry. Sift the flour and salt into a mixing bowl. Add the lard and butter and rub the fats into the flour with your fingertips until the mixture resembles fine breadcrumbs. Stir in enough water – 2 to 3 tablespoons – to make a soft but not sticky dough. Wrap the dough in greaseproof paper and chill it for 20 minutes.

Set the oven at moderately hot (190 C, 375F, gas 5). Place a baking sheet in the oven to heat. Meanwhile, prepare the filling. Beat the potato with the eggs until smooth, then whisk in the milk and cheese. Melt the butter in a pan, add the onion and cook until soft and golden. Add the ham or bacon and fry over medium heat, stirring, for 2 minutes. Cool.

Roll out the dough on a floured surface and use to line a 23-cm/9-in flan case. Spoon the onion mixture into the pastry case and spread it evenly. Pour over the potato mixture. Place the flan on the hot baking sheet and bake in the heated oven for 25 minutes, or until firm and golden brown. Serve warm.
Serves 4–6

Teatime Treats

Don't be put off by the thought of a cake made with mashed potato – it tastes surprisingly good, with a light, moist texture and a delicious flavour. And potatoes make your favourite teatime treats altogether more nutritious because they contain fibre, vitamin C and the B group vitamins. Also, a boiled potato has just 22 calories per ounce, whereas an ounce of plain white flour has 98 calories.

The Czech Almond Cake recipe is a very old, traditional one which is particularly good and rather unusual; definitely worth a try. Children will have great fun making Coconut Ice and Rum Truffles, to give as Christmas gifts or for school fetes. And the Roquefort Bread, served warm with butter, is ideal with soups and spreads, or is delicious just eaten by itself.

Apricot Doughnuts

2 teaspoons dried yeast
150 ml/¼ pint lukewarm milk
225 g/8 oz strong plain flour
2 teaspoons salt
50 g/2 oz butter
175 g/6 oz caster sugar
225 g/8 oz mashed potato
12 almond halves
1 (411-g/14½-oz) can apricot halves
1 teaspoon ground cinnamon
oil for deep frying

Dissolve the yeast in the warm milk and leave to stand for about 10 minutes, or until frothy. Sift the flour with the salt into a bowl and rub in the butter until the mixture resembles fine breadcrumbs. Stir in 50 g/2 oz of the caster sugar. Gradually stir the yeast liquid into the mashed potato, then work in the flour mixture to form a soft but not sitcky dough. Knead on a floured board for 5 minutes, until smooth. Place the dough in a greased bowl, cover and leave to rise in a warm place for 1 hour, or until doubled in size. Then knead the dough for a further 2 minutes.

Divide the dough into 12 pieces. Sandwich each almond half between 2 apricot halves, then enclose each apricot in dough to form a small ball. Leave the doughnuts to rise on a floured baking tray for 30 minutes. Mix the remaining sugar and the cinnamon together in a paper bag. Heat oil to 185 C/360F and fry the doughnuts for 5 to 6 minutes, turning occasionally; you will need to do this in two or three batches. Toss the doughnuts in the sugar mixture and leave to cool. *Makes 12*

Variation

Replace the apricots and almonds with a little raspberry or strawberry jam.

Ginger Nut Biscuits

50 g/2 oz sieved cooked potato
100 g/4 oz butter
175 g/6 oz soft brown sugar
175 g/6 oz plain flour
50 g/2 oz chopped mixed nuts
1 teaspoon ground ginger

Set the oven at moderate (180 C, 350 F, gas 4) and grease two baking sheets. Cream the potato, butter and sugar together until soft and creamy. Then fold in the flour, nuts and ginger – the mixture should form a soft but not sticky dough. Roll out the mixture 5 mm/$\frac{1}{4}$ in thick on a floured surface, then cut it into rounds with a 6-cm/2$\frac{1}{2}$-in biscuit cutter. Place the rounds on the prepared baking sheets and bake in the heated oven for 15 minutes, until golden.

Remove the baking trays from the oven and let the biscuits cool for a few minutes before transferring them to cooling racks. *Makes 16*

Variations

Date and Ginger Wholewheat Biscuits

50 g/2 oz sieved cooked potato
100 g/4 oz butter
150 g/5 oz soft brown sugar
175 g/6 oz wholewheat flour
25 g/1 oz chopped dates
25 g/1 oz crystallised ginger, chopped

Follow the method given above, folding the dates and ginger into the mixture with the flour. *Makes 16*

Rich Ginger Biscuits

50 g/2 oz sieved cooked potato
100 g/4 oz butter
75 g/3 oz soft brown sugar
1 tablespoon golden syrup
50 g/2 oz chopped dates
25 g/1 oz crystallised ginger, chopped
1 teaspoon ground ginger

Follow the method given on the left, creaming the syrup into the mixture with the sugar, and adding the dates, chopped ginger and ground ginger with the flour. *Makes 16*

Coconut Ice

(Illustrated on page 96)

This is a good recipe for children to make, and is also useful for school bazaars and Christmas fairs.

175 g/6 oz icing sugar
100 g/4 oz mashed potato
225 g/8 oz desiccated coconut
few drops of pink food colouring

Grease an 18 × 18-cm/7 × 7-in shallow cake tin. Beat the icing sugar into the mashed potato, then beat in the desiccated coconut. Divide the mixture in two and spread one half over the base of the tin. Colour the remaining half pink with the food colouring and spread it over the top. Chill in the refrigerator until firm, then cut into small squares.

Rum Truffles

(Illustrated on page 96)

Small boxes of these truffles make lovely presents at Christmas time, or serve them with coffee after dinner.

100 g/4 oz plain chocolate
100 g/4 oz mashed potato
175 g/6 oz icing sugar
1 tablespoon rum or a few drops of rum essence
chocolate vermicelli

Melt the chocolate in a heatproof basin over a saucepan of hot water, then gradually beat the chocolate into the mashed potato. Cover and allow to stand until cold, then beat in the icing sugar and the rum or rum essence. Refrigerate until firm. Roll the mixture into balls about the size of a walnut. Dip the balls into the vermicelli and place in small paper sweet cases. Store in the refrigerator until required. *Makes 16*

Czech Almond Cake

This is a traditional cake from Czechoslovakia; served with coffee, it is very light and irresistible!

5 eggs, separated
125 g/4½ oz caster sugar
grated rind and juice of ½ lemon
100 g/4 oz cooked potato, cooled and grated
40 g/1½ oz ground almonds
4 tablespoons marmalade
Icing
75 g/3 oz icing sugar
grated rind and juice of ½ lemon

Set the oven at moderate (180 C, 350 F, gas 4). Grease two 18-cm/7-in sandwich tins and line the bases with greased greaseproof paper. Whisk the egg yolks with the sugar until very thick and light. Gently fold in the lemon rind and juice, followed by the potato. Stiffly beat the egg whites and fold into the mixture with the ground almonds. Spoon or pour the mixture into the prepared tins and level the top. Bake in the preheated oven for 25 to 30 minutes, until golden and firm to the touch. Then turn out on to a wire rack and allow to cool.

Sandwich the cakes together with the marmalade. To make the icing, mix the icing sugar with the lemon rind and juice and add enough boiling water – 2 to 3 teaspoons – to make a smooth, spreadable glacé icing. Pour the icing over the cake and spread to cover evenly. *Serves 6*

Carrot Pudding with Custard

50 g/2 oz sultanas
50 g/2 oz raisins
50 g/2 oz currants
75 g/3 oz finely grated raw potato, drained
½ teaspoon bicarbonate of soda
75 g/3 oz finely grated raw carrot
50 g/2 oz caster sugar
50 g/2 oz soft dark brown sugar
50 g/2 oz plain flour
pinch of salt
1 teaspoon baking powder
1 teaspoon ground ginger
25 g/1 oz butter, softened
Custard
300 ml/½ pint creamy milk
25–50 g/1–2 oz caster sugar
1 vanilla bean or a few drops of vanilla essence
2 egg yolks
2 teaspoons cornflour

Grease a 600-ml/1-pint pudding basin. Cover the sultanas, raisins and currants with hot water and leave to soak for 5 minutes, then drain and reserve. Mix together the potato, bicarbonate of soda and carrot and reserve. Sift the sugars, flour, salt, baking powder and ginger into a large mixing bowl. Add the drained fruit and the potato mixture, then add the softened butter. Beat with a wooden spoon until well mixed. Turn into the prepared basin and cover with a circle of greased greaseproof paper and then with a circle of foil which has been pleated to allow the pudding to rise. Tie securely with string and steam the pudding for 2 hours, on a trivet or upturned saucer, in a pan half-filled with boiling water; add more boiling water to the pan as necessary.

To make the custard, put the milk into a pan with the sugar and the vanilla bean if using (if using vanilla essence this is added at a later stage). Heat until just below boiling point, then discard the vanilla bean. Mix the egg yolks with the cornflour and whisk in the hot milk. Return this mixture to the pan and heat gently, stirring constantly with a wooden spoon, until the mixture thickens; do not allow the mixture to boil. Add the vanilla essence, if using. Turn out the pudding on to a serving dish and serve with custard. *Serves 4–6*

Cheese and Celery Scones

175 g/6 oz plain flour
2 teaspoons baking powder
$\frac{1}{4}$ teaspoon salt
50 g/2 oz cooked potato, sieved
25 g/1 oz butter
25 g/1 oz Parmesan cheese, finely grated
1 stick celery, finely chopped
2–3 tablespoons milk
beaten egg or milk to glaze

Sift together the flour, baking powder and salt into a bowl. Rub in the potato and butter until the mixture resembles fine breadcrumbs. Stir in the cheese and celery, then enough milk to make a soft but not sticky dough. Knead very lightly on a floured board and roll out 1 cm/$\frac{1}{2}$ in thick. Cut into 5-cm/2-in rounds using a plain cutter.

Set the oven at hot (220 C, 425 F, gas 7). Place the scones on a greased baking sheet and glaze them with beaten egg or milk. Bake in the heated oven for 15 minutes. Serve, hot or warm, with butter and cheese or with cold meats and salads. *Makes 8*

Apple Scone

(Illustrated on page 96)

100 g/4 oz plain flour
2 teaspoons baking powder
generous pinch of salt
100 g/4 oz cooked potato, sieved
15 g/½ oz butter
50 g/2 oz caster sugar
3 dessert apples, peeled and cored
2 tablespoons milk
4 tablespoons apricot jam, warmed

Set the oven at moderately hot (200 C, 400 F, gas 6). Sift the flour with the baking powder and salt, then add the potato and butter. Quickly rub in the potato and butter until the mixture resembles fine breadcrumbs. Stir in the sugar. Finely chop one of the apples and stir it into the mixture. Gradually add the milk to give a soft but not sticky dough. Gently knead the dough on a floured board until smooth.

Roll out the dough into a 15-cm/6-in circle, 1-cm/½-in thick. Place on a greased baking sheet. Thinly slice the remaining apples and arrange the slices in circles on top of the scone. Brush with the warmed jam and bake in the heated oven for about 20 minutes, or until golden. Cool slightly and serve warm, with butter. *Serves 6*

Fudge Ring

(Illustrated on page 96)

2 teaspoons dried yeast
150 ml/¼ pint lukewarm milk
225 g/8 oz strong plain flour
½ teaspoon salt
50 g/2 oz butter
225 g/8 oz cooked potato, sieved
2 Mars bars, thinly sliced
50 g/2 oz flaked almonds
icing sugar for dusting

Dissolve the yeast in the warm milk and leave to stand for about 10 minutes, or until frothy. Sift the flour with the salt into a warmed bowl and rub in the butter until the mixture resembles fine breadcrumbs. Stir the yeast liquid into the potato, make a well in the flour mixture and add the potato yeast mixture. Gradually work the flour mixture to make a soft but not sitcky dough. Knead on a floured board for 5 minutes, until smooth. Place the dough in a greased bowl, cover and leave to rise in a warm place for 1 hour, or until doubled in size. Then knead the dough for a further 2 minutes.

Set the oven at moderately hot (200 C, 400 F, gas 6). Divide the dough into three portions and roll each into a rectangle measuring 50 × 6 cm/20 × 2½ in. Place slices of Mars bar down the centre of each strip, then bring the dough up round the filling to enclose. Pinch to seal firmly, then pinch the ends of the three rolls together as if about to plait them. Twist the rolls together.

Butter a 1.4-litre/2½-pint ring tin and sprinkle it with the almonds. Put the twisted dough into the prepared tin, joining the ends. Cover and leave to rise for 30 minutes, or until doubled in size. Bake the ring in the heated oven for 30 minutes, then turn out on to a cooling rack and leave to cool. Serve the same day, dusted with icing sugar. *Serves 6*

Banana Nut Loaf

100 g/4 oz butter
175 g/6 oz soft light brown sugar
2 eggs, lightly beaten
100 g/4 oz plain flour
generous pinch of salt
2 teaspoons baking powder
50 g/2 oz dried apricots, chopped
100 g/4 oz walnuts, chopped
450 g/1 lb ripe bananas, peeled and mashed
100 g/4 oz cooked potato, sieved

Set the oven at moderate (160 C, 325F, gas 3) and grease a
1-kg/2-lb loaf tin. Cream the butter and sugar and gradually
beat in the beaten eggs. Sift the flour with the salt and baking
powder and fold into the mixture with the apricots and walnuts.
Mash the bananas and potato together and stir into the mixture.
When well mixed spoon into the prepared tin and level the top.
Bake in the preheated oven for 1½ hours, or until a skewer
inserted into the centre of the loaf comes out clean. Cool in the
tin, then turn out and wrap. Keep for two to three days before
serving with butter. *Makes 1*

Chocolate Pudding with Chocolate Sauce

This pudding is amazingly light, and definitely more-ish!

100 g / 4 oz butter
100 g / 4 oz caster sugar
2 eggs, beaten
25 g / 1 oz cocoa powder
1 teaspoon baking powder
100 g / 4 oz cooked potato, sieved
50 g / 2 oz ground almonds
Sauce
150 ml / $\frac{1}{4}$ pint single cream
100 g / 4 oz plain chocolate

Grease a 1.15-litre/2-pint pudding basin. Cream the butter and sugar until light and fluffy. Gradually beat in the eggs, beating well after each addition. Sift the cocoa powder and baking powder together and gently fold into the mixture, then fold in the sieved potato and the ground almonds. Turn the mixture into the prepared basin and cover with a circle of greased greaseproof paper and then with a circle of foil which has been pleated to allow the pudding to rise. Tie securely with string and steam the pudding for $1\frac{1}{2}$ hours, on a trivet or upturned saucer, in a pan half-filled with boiling water; add more boiling water to the pan as necessary. When the pudding is cooked, remove the basin from the pan and leave to stand for 5 minutes. Turn out on to a dish and serve immediately, with the hot chocolate sauce.

To make the sauce, bring the cream to the boil in a pan, then remove from the heat. Break the chocolate into pieces and add to the cream, stirring until smooth and melted. *Serves 4*

Roquefort Bread

2 teaspoons dried yeast
150 ml/¼ pint lukewarm milk
450 g/1 lb strong plain flour
2 teaspoons salt
25 g/1 oz butter
225 g/8 oz cooked potato, sieved
100 g/4 oz Roquefort or blue cheese, crumbled
beaten egg to glaze

Dissolve the yeast in the warm milk and leave to stand for about 10 minutes, or until frothy. Sift the flour with the salt into a warmed bowl and rub in the butter until the mixture resembles fine breadcrumbs. Stir the yeast liquid into the potato then work this mixture into the flour to make a soft but not sticky dough. Knead on a floured board for 5 minutes, then transfer to an oiled bowl. Cover and leave to rise in a warm place for 1 hour, or until doubled in size. Then knead again for 1 minute and knead in the crumbled cheese.

Grease a 450-g/1-lb loaf tin and set the oven at moderately hot (200 C, 400 F, gas 6). Shape the dough to fit the tin, then leave the dough to rise in the tin in a warm place for 30 minutes, or until doubled in size. Brush the loaf with beaten egg and bake it in the heated oven for 15 minutes. Reduce the temperature to moderate (180 C, 350 F, gas 4) and bake for a further 15 minutes. Turn out the loaf and leave to cool. The bread is also delicious toasted. *Makes 1 loaf*

Fresh Herb and Garlic Rolls

2 teaspoons dried yeast
150 ml/¼ pint lukewarm milk
pinch of sugar
450 g/1 lb strong plain flour
2 teaspoons salt
75 g/3 oz butter
225 g/8 oz cooked potato, sieved
1 tablespoon chopped chives
1 tablespoon chopped parsley
1 teaspoon chopped marjoram
pinch of black pepper
6 cloves garlic, or to taste, crushed
beaten egg to glaze
kibbled wheat

Dissolve the yeast in the warm milk, add the sugar and leave to stand for 10–15 minutes, until frothy. Sift the flour with the salt into a warmed bowl and rub in 25 g/1 oz of the butter until the mixture resembles fine breadcrumbs. Stir the yeast liquid into the potato, then work this mixture into the flour to make a soft sticky dough (it may be necessary to add a few tablespoons of lukewarm water). Knead on a floured board for 5 minutes, then transfer to an oiled bowl. Cover and leave to rise for 1 hour, or until doubled in size. Allow the remaining butter to soften.

In a small bowl, combine the softened butter, fresh herbs, pepper and garlic. Mix until well blended, then chill.

Divide the dough into eight. Knead each portion into a roll shape, make a hole in the centre and fill with a knob of the garlic butter. Knead the mixture until the garlic butter is in the centre of the roll. Repeat with each roll. Leave to prove for a further 10 minutes, or until the rolls have doubled their size.

Brush the rolls with the beaten egg and sprinkle some kibbled wheat on the top. Bake in a moderately hot oven (200 C, 400 F, gas 6) for 15 to 20 minutes, or until the rolls are golden and firm. Turn out on to a wire rack to cool. *Makes 8*

Index

INDEX